A Culinary History of SOUTHERN DELAWARE

A Culinary History of
SOUTHERN DELAWARE

Scrapple, Beach Plums and Muskrat

Denise Clemons

AMERICAN PALATE

Published by American Palate
A Division of The History Press
Charleston, SC
www.historypress.net

First published 2016

Manufactured in the United States

ISBN 978.1.46713.546.7

Library of Congress Control Number: 2016933578

Notice: The information in this book is true and complete to the best of our knowledge. It is offered without guarantee on the part of the author or The History Press. The author and The History Press disclaim all liability in connection with the use of this book.

*To Jack, for his love and support during our many adventures together—
and for always offering to wash the dishes.*

CONTENTS

ACKNOWLEDGEMENTS

While writing is a solitary occupation, these words and photographs could not have come to the page without the invaluable assistance of my husband, Jack.

I am indebted to the people of Southern Delaware who have given me insight into their lives and their histories, especially the Bennett family of Frankford.

The history of the state of Delaware is expertly organized and easily accessible in the welcoming space of the Delaware Public Archives.

I would like to thank members of my *Cape Gazette* newspaper family, especially my editor, Jen Ellingsworth, who supported my explorations into the favorite foods of Southern Delaware.

The extraordinary memory and extensive library of Lewes historian Hazel Brittingham helped enliven the portrayal of Sussex County.

Finally, I am grateful to Hannah Cassilly and her team at Arcadia Publishing and The History Press for their guidance and support in completing this project.

INTRODUCTION

Welcome to Southern Delaware! Today's travels on local roads may include slow traffic backed up behind a harvester on its way to gather corn, a windshield splashed by an irrigator spraying across the edge of a field or the daunting experience of driving behind a chicken truck scattering feathers like snowflakes on a trip to the processing plant.

From the Native Americans who originally inhabited the region to the farm-to-table trends popular today, Southern Delaware has always been connected to the bounty of the land and sea. With the arrival of European settlers in the seventeenth century through the subsequent population expansion, tools and techniques for farming and fishing were modernized. However, most of the culinary traditions have changed very little over the years.

With a geography that separates this area from northern towns and neighboring states, and with a robust population tracing its history back to a handful of founding families, Southern Delaware is unique. Considered part of the Delmarva Peninsula, yet with a different personality than Maryland, Virginia or cities in the northern parts of the state, this tidy patch of land quilted with waterways has a story all its own.

Southern Delaware is dotted with small-town centers and lined with ever-growing coastal beach communities. The balance of the area is agricultural—poultry farms, vineyards, orchards, dairies and acres upon acres of cropland. A few years ago, almost half the acreage in Southern Delaware was farmland, and despite aggressive building projects for housing

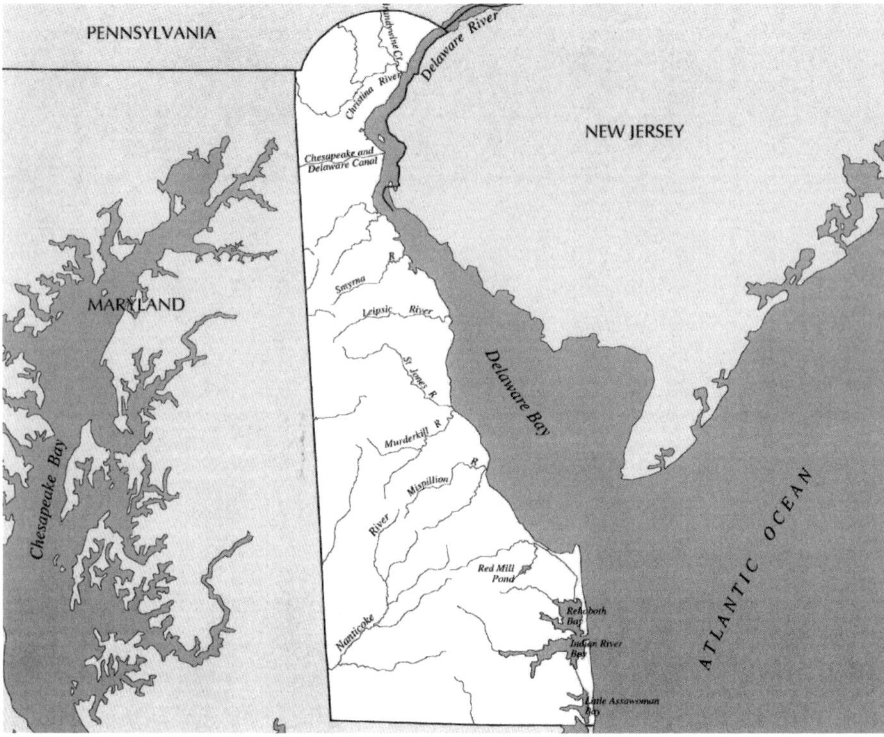

Delaware state map showing the vast network of waterways in Southern Delaware.

developments and expansion of shopping centers, the nature of the region remains tied to agriculture.

Early maps of the region were less frequently labeled with specific town names and more often marked with the family name associated with each farm, mill or waterway landing. Often those names persisted, either as official names of a place or in the affectionate memories of the current residents.

These pages illustrate the same varieties of fish and fowl that fed the native Nanticoke tribes and remain an integral part of the modern diet, sometimes with very little embellishment. Fortunate to have a climate favorable for cultivating a range of flora and fauna, the culinary history of Southern Delaware is entwined in the growth and decline and resurgent demand for key food crops and the dishes in which they star.

Almost every one of Delaware's "official" designations is connected to food:

- Official State Beverage: milk
- Official State Bird: blue hen chicken

- Official State Dessert: peach pie
- Official State Fish: weakfish
- Official State Flower: peach blossom
- Official State Fruit: strawberries
- Official State Seal: sheaf of wheat, ear of corn, ox

One of the discoveries in my journey through the culinary history of Southern Delaware is how infrequently historians documented exactly what people were eating. Perhaps because eating is such an essential and automatic activity, the repetitive contents of regular meals must have seemed completely unremarkable to the chroniclers of more momentous events. A few descriptions written by early settlers in the region and some of the first cookbooks available in America help illustrate the origins of many local culinary traditions. The balance of the details about foods on the menu is found in descriptions of agricultural practices, family histories and the treasured recipes that were passed from generation to generation.

In this collection, you will discover many of the traditional foods native to Southern Delaware, as well as insights into how those foods were harvested, preserved, traded and enjoyed. Not every vegetable or every species of fish will be detailed, but those that were (and still are) popular in the region appear, along with a sampling of recipes from the past as well as today.

A combination of climate and geography joined to give Southern Delaware the natural resources for its unique flavors. The culinary history of Southern Delaware is a tale of people and place. From scrapple to beach plums, peaches to muskrat, the best from local farmers and fishermen is always on the table in Southern Delaware.

Chapter 1

SETTLING SOUTHERN DELAWARE

THE FIRST TOWN IN THE FIRST STATE

The Dutch were the first European settlers to arrive in Southern Delaware. They came in search of whaling trade opportunities in 1631 and called the area Zwaanendael, or "Valley of the Swans." This small group of men built an enclosed fort in what became the town of Lewes on the tip of land between the Atlantic Ocean and the Delaware Bay. According to the evidence left behind, they did not develop friendly relations with the original inhabitants they encountered. Not only did they fail to find whales in the coastal waters, but their entire enterprise also came to an untimely end in a dispute stemming from a cultural misunderstanding with the local Native Americans. When Peter de Vries arrived a year later to check on the settlement, he found that his men had been killed and the buildings burned.

While their presence was short-lived, this timely arrival of the Dutch predated several other land grants and property claims. In the years leading up to the Revolutionary War, ownership was variously held by settlers from Sweden, England and Holland. The last was William Penn's attempt to include the "lower counties" within the borders of Pennsylvania. The issue was finally resolved during negotiations prior to the start of the Continental Congress, and the three counties (New Castle, Kent and Sussex) became the independent state of Delaware.

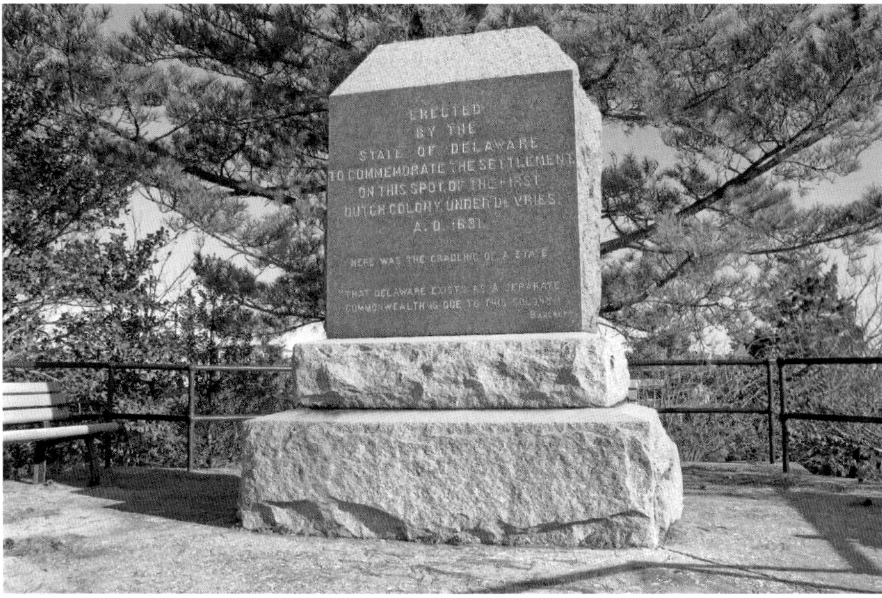

The De Vries monument on Pilottown Road, Lewes, Delaware, marks the site of the state's first settlement and Delaware's sovereignty as a separate state. *Jack Clemons photo.*

Other early claims by the English, who wanted the region as part of the Virginia territory, left their mark in Delaware's name, which comes from the title of the first Virginia governor, Thomas West, 3rd Baron de la Warr. As the first of the original thirteen colonies to ratify the constitution of the new country in 1787, Delaware earned its nickname of the "First State." Lewes, in the heart of southern Delaware, has come to be known as the "First Town in the First State."

Progress came slowly to Southern Delaware. As late as 1860, Kent and Sussex Counties remained isolated from the rest of the surrounding region to the north and west. Harold Hancock described this leisurely rural lifestyle in his book *Delaware During the Civil War.* He found that most people lived on their family farms or in small communities; roads were sandy, not paved; oxen pulled crude farm machinery; much of the harvest was sown and harvested by hand; fabric was loomed from handspun, vegetable-dyed flax; and foodstuffs were limited to what was grown on the farm, pulled from local waters and culled from nearby forests.

After the Civil War, the residents of Southern Delaware became more involved in commercial growing and distribution of fruit, vegetables and grain crops. Over time, the roads and railroads improved transportation, while modernization of machinery and techniques created opportunities for commercial sales and food processing for distant markets.

Throughout the centuries, the favorite foods of Southern Delaware have changed very little; the residents of small towns and expanding communities of today share a rich culinary history.

THE NANTICOKES

Long before any European explorers found their way to the North American continent, Southern Delaware was home to a thriving native population of Nanticoke Indians, descendants of whom still live here today. One of the earliest explorers in the region, Captain John Smith, the founder of Jamestown Colony, extensively traveled the waterways and made several observations about the Nanticokes, whose name translates as "the Tidewater People." In his 1608 journey along the Nanticoke River, he observed the farming, fishing and hunting practices of the group. He described them as the "best merchants" of all the tribes he encountered, trading animal pelts and beads fashioned from clam and oyster shells.

Because of their proximity to the water, seafood was the primary protein in the Nanticoke diet. Using spears, specially designed woven baskets, nets or bow and arrows, they successfully caught crab, eel, shrimp and a variety of fin fish, especially shad, which were eaten roasted or boiled. They feasted on the abundant supplies of oysters and clams, both raw and cooked. The women butchered the deer, elk, muskrat, rabbit, turkey and ducks hunted by the men. Meat was spit roasted, smoked or added to stews and broths. According to tradition, some of the meat was dried, pounded into a powder and mixed with melted animal fat to make pemmican, a long-lasting, high-energy food that can be considered a precursor to our modern protein bar.

Although the marshy region was not well suited for agriculture, areas slightly inland were cultivated as farmland, where the "three sisters" were grown: corn, squash and beans. Cornstalks provided a trellis for the beans, and the spreading squash vines suppressed weeds at the base of the plants. Fruits, nuts and berries were staples of the Nanticoke diet, although they were rarely eaten fresh out of hand. Fruit and berry pulp was boiled into a dense mash that was then dried into well-preserved

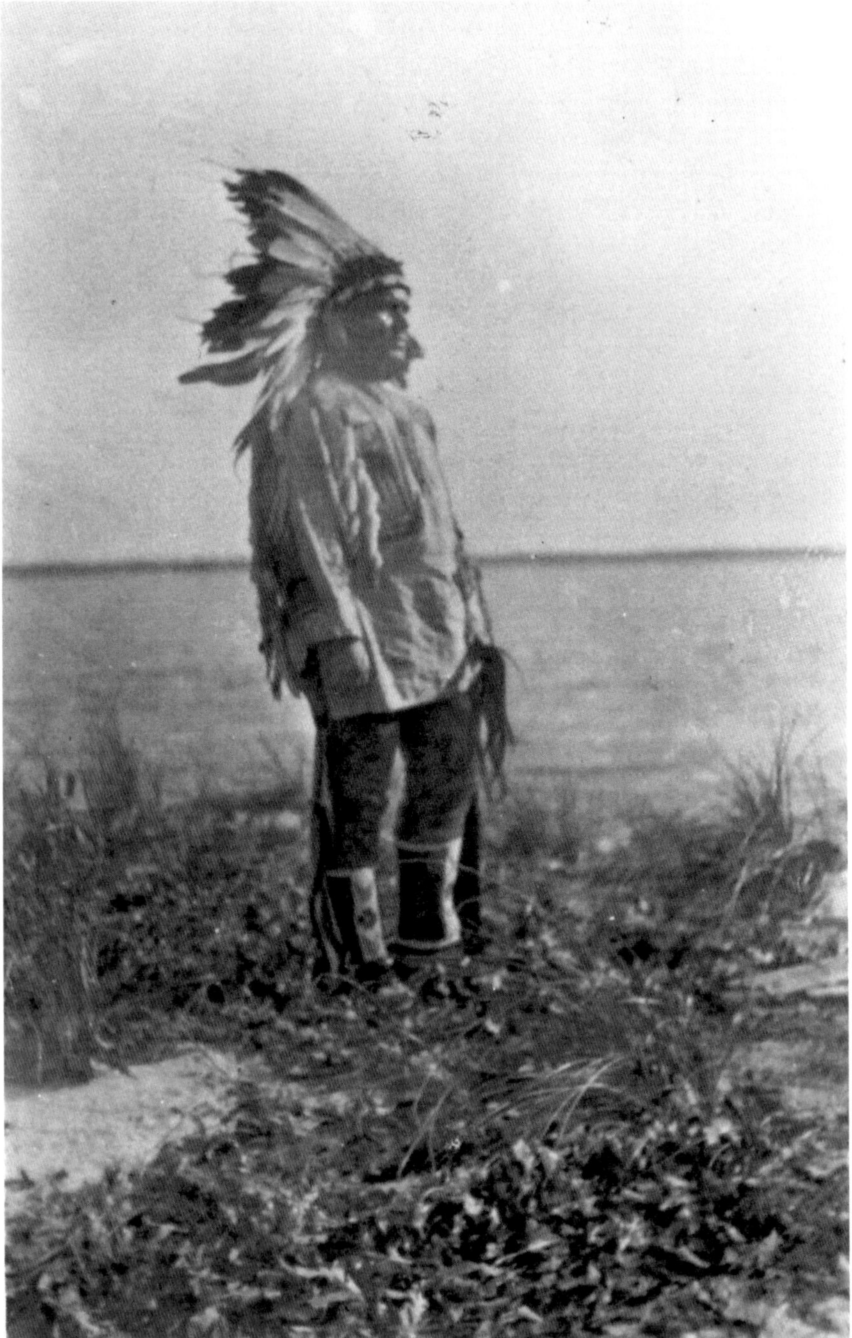

Nanticoke man in tribal dress at a powwow, circa 1920. *Courtesy of the Delaware Public Archives.*

strips of "fruit leather." Nuts were shelled and boiled so the fat that floated to the top could be skimmed and saved to prepare other dishes. The nut pulp was used for fried pancakes, and the reserved boiling liquid was used to cook corn grits.

Everything we bring to the table in Southern Delaware stems from the traditions handed down from the first people who lived here. They shared what they knew about netting, snaring, shooting, trapping, planting and harvesting, giving early settlers insight into their successful techniques. And they knew how to recycle and reuse: discarded fish bones became fertilizer, and corn husks became livestock bedding.

There are no cookbooks describing how to make the corn and meat dishes favored by the Nanticokes—only traditions passed down through generations. With nothing written as a reference, children learned from their parents by observing and practicing. Into the late seventeenth and early eighteenth centuries, the traditional methods of cooking that had served the Nanticokes for generations evolved with the influx of European settlers. As the Nanticoke community sold off parts of their tribal lands to the newcomers, they were more limited in the available supply of fresh fish and game; many residents turned to farming and trapping to feed their families.

When asked today about their food traditions, the members of the Nanticoke tribe living in Southern Delaware will list three things: corn, muskrat and fry bread. If you were to attend a local powwow, their annual tribal reunion celebration, you would find tacos made with fresh rounds of fry bread and authentic pemmican from dried meat, fat and berries.

RECIPES

These are modern versions of two traditional Nanticoke foods.

Johnnycakes

Once cooked, these sturdy cornmeal disks could be packed to take along on a trip, which gave them the nickname "journey cakes." Instead of the long-handled wooden tool used to hold these over the fire to brown, the modern cook can use a skillet or griddle to cook these on the stove. On today's menu, these are a nice change from pancakes for breakfast and tasty when served with maple syrup or jam.

1 cup cornmeal
¾ teaspoon salt
1 cup water
½ cup milk
fat for cooking

Combine the cornmeal and salt in a bowl; set aside. Bring the water to a boil and pour slowly over the cornmeal while stirring constantly. Stir in the milk until mixture is smooth. Generously grease a skillet with bacon fat or lard and place over medium-high heat. When the pan is hot, spoon dollops of batter into the pan and flatten each round to about ¼-inch thick. Cook until golden brown and then flip to brown the other side.

Fry Bread

A byproduct of the forced relocation of Native Americans onto reservations during the 1800s. With limited (and sometimes spoiled) rations provided by the government, women made this high-calorie, puffed-dough circle from just a few ingredients. Their original version might have used dried milk powder, but buttermilk adds a lighter texture. Resist the temptation to substitute vegetable oil—you need to fry these in a traditional solid shortening such as Crisco.

1½ cups flour
1½ teaspoons baking powder
¼ teaspoon salt
½ cup buttermilk
¼ cup water (or more, as needed)
solid shortening for cooking

Sift together the flour, baking powder and salt in a large mixing bowl. Make a well in the center and add buttermilk, stirring to combine. Add just enough water for the dough to hold together, but do not overwork. Cover bowl with a dishtowel and set aside for 45 minutes. Melt enough shortening in a skillet to reach a depth of two inches. Break off a piece of dough about the size of a lime. Set it on a flat work surface and flatten, pushing outward from the center to a diameter of about five inches. Slide disk into the hot oil and cook until browned on the bottom, about 1 minute. Using a pair of tongs, flip the dough and cook until browned on the other side, about another minute. Remove to a paper towel to drain; continue until all the dough has been cooked. Serve topped with honey, cinnamon sugar or jam; alternatively, use as a soft taco shell and top with seasoned ground meat, salsa and cheese. Yield: 6 servings.

Chapter 2

FARMERS FIRST AND ALWAYS

The lands and waters of Southern Delaware attracted European immigrants who could readily earn their livelihoods and feed their families by farming and fishing, a lifestyle that continues through today.

EARLY DAYS

From the time of the first European settlers to the mid-twentieth century, most families who lived in Southern Delaware were farmers and fishermen. Their diets were limited to the crops they grew, the livestock they pastured, the game they hunted and the fish they caught. During the 1600s, families cultivated corn, peas, wheat and barley, all of which grew well in the region. They arrived from Europe or relocated from nearby Virginia and Maryland, bringing pigs, cattle, sheep and goats, which they raised for both meat and milk.

By the early 1700s, tobacco was still popular as a literal cash crop: harvests were used to settle debts, pay court fines or exchange for purchases. Beef cattle ranged freely across the marshes and in the woodlands, needing almost four years to grow large enough for slaughter. By comparison, according to the Delaware Department of Agriculture, today's commercial beef producers grow their cattle to full size in less than one year.

In this period, many of the farms were small, producing just enough to feed the family, with some surplus to sell or trade for commodities and imported goods such as sugar and spices. Life revolved around the schedule of the growing season: preparing the ground after the spring thaw, planting crops, thinning and weeding the fields and, finally, harvesting.

A similar cycle dictated when hogs were fattened, butchered and cured with salt or smoke or both. In the winter months, hunting and trapping augmented the menu of smoked meats, preserved fruit and pickled vegetables. While most livestock and game became part of a meal according to the season, hens supplied eggs throughout the year.

The daily diet of the region was simple and spare. For most people who rose early to begin chores, breakfast was a hastily swallowed bowl of cornmeal mush or bread soaked in milk, typically washed down with cider or beer. The main meal of the day, called dinner, was served in the early afternoon. Meat or fish, roasted or stewed, was a common main course, served with boiled vegetables and bread. An evening meal was most likely leftovers from earlier in the day or the previous day.

Plates, known as trenchers, were made of wood or horn, and a small, shallow, one-handled cup known as a porringer served for eating pudding or drinking soup. Spoons were much flatter than the deep, bowl-shaped spoons of today, and the first forks (rarely used) were also flat, with only two tines. Many of the more religious of the early residents believed that their food should be simple, not indulgent or fancy; much of what they ate was boiled into stews or roasted on a spit over the fire.

Meals were prepared at the main hearth, located in the largest room of the house, or at an outside fireplace during warmer months. In some homes, the kitchen was built as a separate, small building or a lean-to structure attached to the house. Without refrigerators or pantries, various areas in the house were used to preserve and store different types of food—smokehouse for meats, root cellar or other cool storage for vegetables and the attic for dried beans and fruits.

MIDDLE YEARS

Toward the end of the century, tobacco had declined in importance due to the labor-intensive nature of its cultivation, and grain crops started to gain in popularity and profit. Innovation in milling technology, specifically the invention of the automated gristmill, allowed farmers in Southern Delaware to supply flour to markets throughout the northeast region of the newly independent nation.

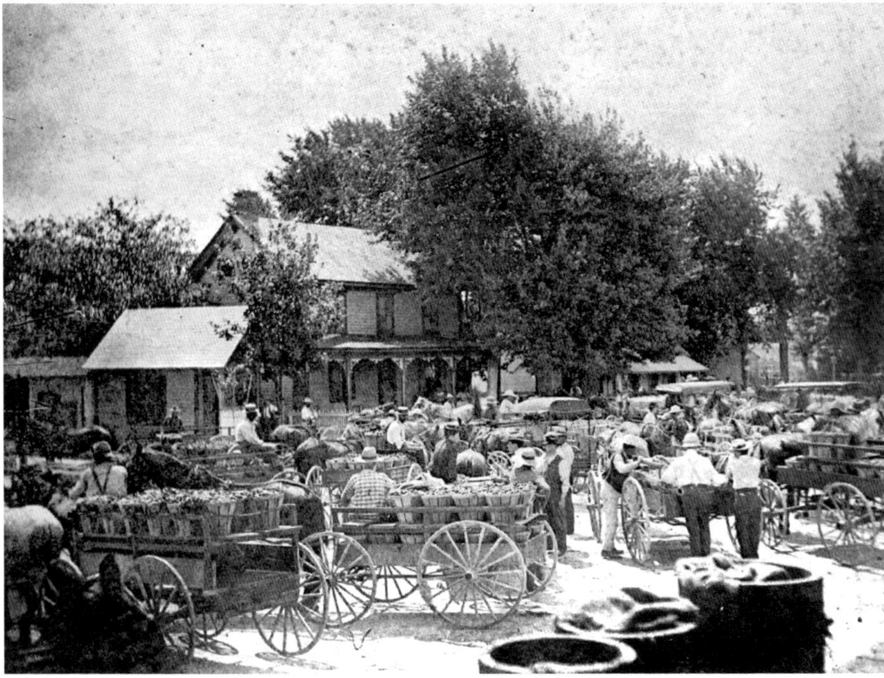

Wagons loaded with baskets of Delaware peaches arrive at the market exchange to meet buyers and brokers. *Courtesy of the Delaware Public Archives.*

Roads were rutted and truck travel arduous, so much of the harvest was shipped by boat. During the 1800s, improved means of transportation helped the farmer reach new markets. No longer limited to the steamboats on the many north–south waterways, the Chesapeake and Delaware Canal opened in 1829, providing an east–west route from the Atlantic Ocean to the Chesapeake Bay. This was closely followed by the expansion of the Delaware Railroad, which finally reached the southern border of the state in 1859.

Since the mid-1800s, a wide range of foods was supplied by the growers in Southern Delaware. The production of unprecedented tonnages set national records for both peaches in 1875 and strawberries in 1935. Dozens of canneries opened across the region, preserving vegetables, fruits and seafood for distant markets served by familiar names like Heinz and Campbell. The broiler chicken industry emerged in the early twentieth century and continues to thrive today.

At the same time, kitchen technology improved from a central hearth to wood-fired stoves and, eventually, to coal-burning stoves with more efficient

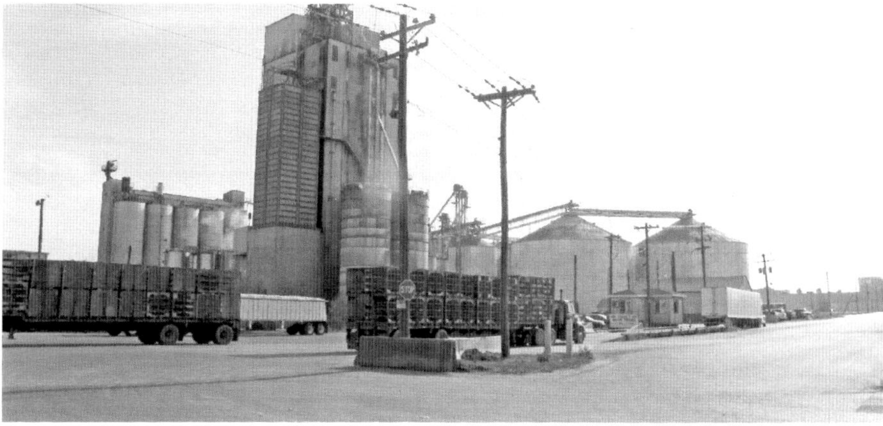

Mountainaire Farms poultry processing complex in Millsboro, Delaware, today. *Jack Clemons photo.*

ovens. Sinks were slow to appear in the farmhouse kitchen; buckets filled at cisterns and wells were hand-carried to the house for washing, cooking and drinking as late as the early twentieth century. Electrical service and sanitation initiatives were first seen in the larger towns and more densely populated areas, and some farms didn't have running water or electricity until after the end of World War I.

And we have come full circle. At first, the only foods available were locally sourced. As technology advanced to preserve the harvest by canning and freezing, transportation improvements provided more efficient distribution networks. Through the end of the twentieth century, convenience became paramount, and many crops were bred for features such as sturdiness to keep them intact during shipping instead of offering consumers better texture and superior flavor.

In today's world of "slow food" and "farm-to-fork" trends, local sources are again celebrated. Oddly shaped heirloom tomatoes are prized over the perfectly symmetrical and completely tasteless hothouse varieties. Neglected vegetables such as Brussels sprouts and cauliflower have become almost faddish in their popularity. Free-range chickens and their cage-free eggs are offered for sale in reused cardboard egg cartons, a badge of honor, attesting to their "natural" origins.

Throughout Southern Delaware, restaurants now list the names of the farms that supplied ingredients for the dishes on their menus. Grocery store chains have discovered that produce is more popular if shoppers see a sign with the grower's name above the bins. Farmers' markets have become ubiquitous. During the summer months, there are dozens of markets in operation throughout the region, and some innovative suppliers operate off-season delivery services and indoor markets for local products.

The Bennett Family: From Salt to Peaches

One of the best ways to illustrate the evolution of the culinary traditions of Southern Delaware is to follow a family who have been working the land for generations. Scattered across the region are almost 130 properties that have been designated as Century Farms. This honor is awarded by the Delaware Department of Agriculture to those families who have successfully farmed at least a portion of the same lands for more than one hundred continuous years. Among them are many names familiar to locals: T.S. Smith, Fifer, Warrington, Miller, Magee, Rogers, Hastings and Bennett, just to list a few.

Bennett Orchards is the current name of the original lands farmed by the ancestors of Jim Bennett in Frankford, Delaware. His wife, Carrie, brought her midwestern farming roots to the family, and their sons, Hail and Henry, are the sixth generation to farm in this location. Their current crops have evolved from a long series of successful ventures, keeping pace with the agricultural trends of the times.

The original family members who settled the area were reported to have arrived by means of a shipwreck on the Indian River inlet in the middle of the eighteenth century, in a place known today as Cotton Patch. Beginning with salt production (through evaporation of seawater), the family was active in agricultural pursuits for many years. One early enterprise was a mill complex, built around 1790. Named the "Baltimore Mills" for its location in the Baltimore Hundred section of Sussex County, the water-powered operation included both a gristmill (for grain) and a sawmill (for lumber).

As the region became more populated, the lumber mill processed timber from cypress trees harvested in the local swamps, while the gristmill ground wheat and rye into flour; the nearby Indian River provided water transportation to Philadelphia and beyond. The mill served the community continually until a hurricane in 1930 destroyed much of the facility.

Nearly one hundred years into the mill's operation, family member Jehu Bennett appears in the Farmers & Fruit Growers section of the 1874–75 *State Directory and Gazetteer*. Based on records of the time, his crops included

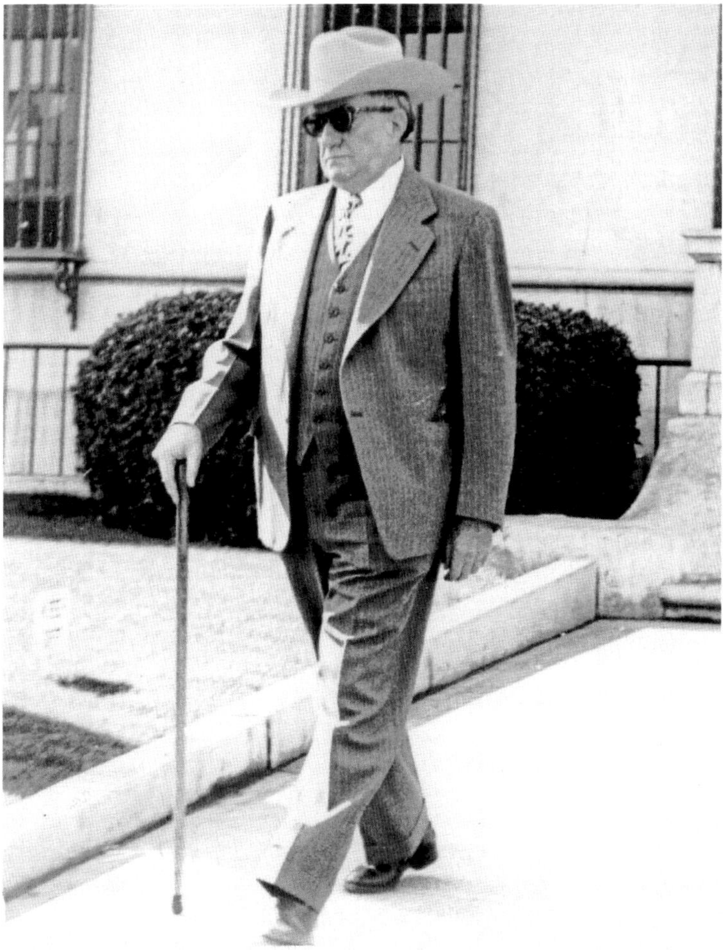

Senator Asa Bennett, circa 1952, the first grower to replace egg-laying hens with broiler chickens at the birth of a new industry. *Courtesy of Bennett Orchards.*

peaches, apples, pears, wheat, corn, sweet potatoes and peas. By the turn of the twentieth century, Jehu's grandson Asa Bennett was managing the farm, as well as beginning his distinguished career in public service.

When the peach industry failed due to a blight that struck the orchards in the 1890s, wise Delaware growers turned to other crops, such as apples and strawberries. Asa Bennett was one of the largest strawberry producers in 1918, and during his terms as a state senator, he gifted many pallets of fresh berries to his colleagues serving in Washington, D.C.

Keeping pace with demand, Asa Bennett built a cider plant to supplement his canning operations for tomatoes, green beans, sweet potatoes and pears. In addition to his diversified approach to farming, Asa Bennett recognized market trends, which made him among the first to enter the lucrative broiler chicken business when disease struck his egg-laying flocks of hens.

The family tradition of farming with a focus on key products continued. Asa's son, James Hail Bennett, worked with his father, and they contributed to the innovations in chicken housing, constructing more efficient long houses instead of multiple, separate small houses. They also began turkey production on the farm, starting the birds inside the protection of the chicken houses before setting them out to range freely. Once they were ready for market, they were transported by truck to be processed for sale.

Several of the original farm buildings are still standing; the old millstone sits at the end of the Bennetts' driveway now, and there are still several row crops growing on the Bennett lands. In 1983, Jim and Carrie Bennett began another experiment. Understanding the characteristics of the sandy, well-drained soil of their farmland inspired them to plant twenty-five acres with peach trees. Implementing scientific cultivation practices for quality fruit

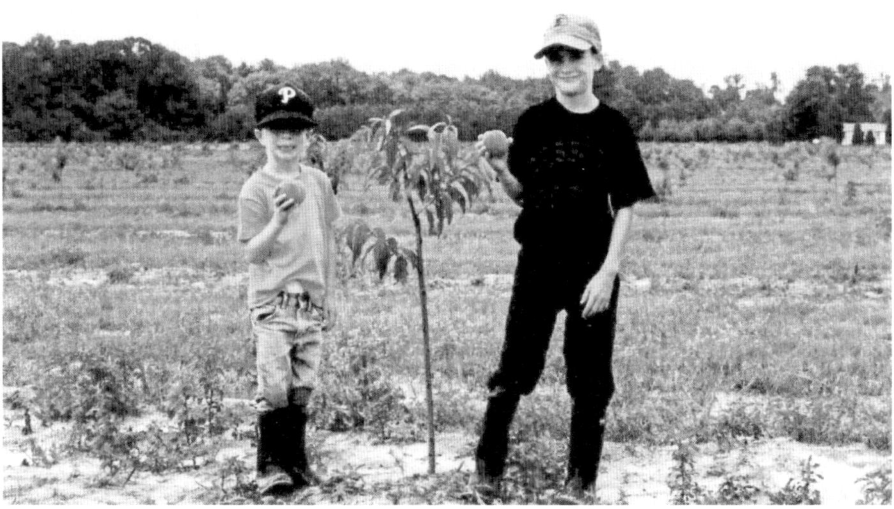

Hail and Henry Bennett, sixth generation of a farming family, admiring a young peach tree, 2009. *Courtesy of Bennett Orchards.*

production, they planned to offer a "pick-your-own" experience to visitors and locals alike.

During the summer peach season, Bennett's loyal customers form long lines at the regional farmers' markets looking for perfectly ripe peaches. Others make the trip to visit the farm's on-site market stand or wander through the orchards to pick their own fresh fruit. Local grocery stores sell Bennett Orchards peaches directly from the signature red baskets in which they are delivered, so shoppers will recognize the familiar source.

A few years ago, following their tradition of innovation, the Bennett family again considered the climate and soil conditions of their farm and planted eight acres of blueberries. In addition to twenty varieties of peaches, they also grow five different types of blueberries that have already become popular with restaurants, groceries and consumers.

As owners of a Century Farm, the Bennett family appreciates the importance of contributing fresh, local food into the supply chain. Over the past ten years, Carrie Bennett has founded two farmers' markets in Sussex County, and the entire family advocates for the protection of Southern Delaware's vast tracts of farmland. On several occasions through the years, when faced with proposals for highway routes that would dissect their family's lands, the members of the Bennett family acted quickly to raise public awareness and gain political support to prevent destruction of centuries of farming traditions. We hope that their family farm will feed us for another hundred years.

RECIPES

Crumb-Top Peach Blueberry Pie

Two fruits from Bennett Orchards under a crumbly topping that delivers all the sweetness of summer.

TOPPING:
¼ cup flour
½ cup cornmeal
¼ cup brown sugar
¼ teaspoon nutmeg
⅓ cup rolled oats
4 tablespoons softened butter

Combine the dry ingredients and cut in the butter with a pastry blender (or pulse in a food processor) until mixture resembles coarse meal. Refrigerate while making the pie.

Pie:
pastry for 9-inch piecrust
5 cups sliced, peeled peaches
1 cup blueberries
1 tablespoon vanilla
1 tablespoon lemon juice
½ cup brown sugar
1 tablespoon flour
2 tablespoons cornstarch
¼ teaspoon nutmeg
¼ teaspoon salt

Preheat oven to 350 F. Line a pie pan with the pastry and crimp the edge around the rim. Combine the peaches, blueberries, vanilla and lemon juice in a mixing bowl; set aside. Whisk together the sugar, flour, cornstarch, nutmeg and salt in a small bowl. Pour the dry ingredients over the fruit and toss to coat thoroughly. Spread the fruit mixture into the crust and dot evenly with the topping. Bake until browned and bubbly, about 1 hour. Allow to cool for 30 minutes before slicing. Yield: 8 servings.

Chapter 3

FRUITS OF THE ORCHARDS AND VINES

The culinary traditions of Southern Delaware are full of sweet and juicy fruits. The native beach plums never became a commercial crop outside the state, while from the outset, strawberries and peaches were transported to markets in Philadelphia and New York through a network of waterways. Commerce was transformed with the construction of railroad lines, which gave perishable fruits a swifter journey from local fields to larger and more distant markets.

Beach Plums

The wild beach plum is found only along the sandy dunes of the North American coast from Maine to Maryland. One of the first native plants encountered by European explorers, both Giovanni de Verrazzano in the sixteenth century and Henry Hudson in 1609 described the showy shrub. In 1785, Henry Marshall's scientific description established its botanical identity and formal name, *Prunus maritima*.

These shrubs are native to Southern Delaware, flourishing on the twenty-nine-mile barrier island between Broadkill Beach and Lewes. Aptly named, Beach Plum Island offers an ideal habitat for the distinctively astringent fruit, which prefers well-drained, sandy soil and full sunlight. Because beach plums tolerate salty winds and cold temperatures, they have thrived in the region for centuries. This particular stretch of sand is now protected as part of the Cape Henlopen State Park.

Beach plum bushes grow in clusters in the lee of the dunes, very close to sea level. Sometimes after windy storms, their gnarled branches appear to be partly buried in the sand. The plants can grow to about five feet high and wide, spreading by underground suckers. They have jagged, egg-shaped leaves and bright-white flower blossoms that appear in May.

These plants were well known to the Native Americans and prized for their sweet-tart flavor. Quite small in size, often less than an inch in diameter, beach plums have a freestone pit much like a cherry. By early September, the small fruits have changed in color from green to pink to maroon and, finally, to deep blue. When ripe, they will be covered with a protective white dust known as "bloom" that helps them retain moisture.

With signature acidity, the fruit is not a good candidate to eat out of hand, but its distinctive tartness has been featured in jellies and jams since colonial times. Making beach plum jelly is not difficult, but it can be challenging for the uninitiated. A combination of red and blue plums is usually selected for the right balance of color and flavor. Standard canning techniques begin

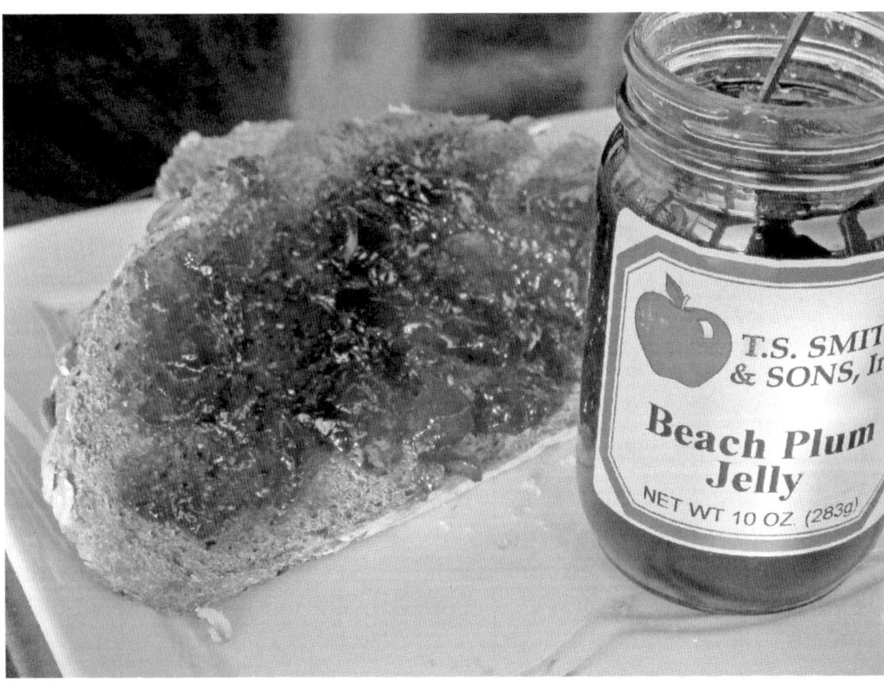

Peach plum jelly from T.S. Smith & Sons, Bridgeville, Delaware. *Jack Clemons photo.*

with boiling and mashing the whole plum (pitting the tiny fruits would be tediously time-consuming). The juice and pulp are strained and then mixed with sugar and pectin in exactingly precise proportions to ensure that the jelly will actually gel. After boiling the mixture, the next step is to fill and seal the canning jars before setting them aside to cool.

Instructions on the process typically include ways to use the un-gelled fruit juice that may result from common measuring mistakes. Substituting sweetened beach plum juice for cranberry juice in colorful cocktails is always at the top of this list, as a puckery flavor profile is found in both fruits. There are confident and capable beach plum jelly producers in several local towns, so unless you know where to harvest beach plums, it might be best to buy the jelly already made.

Like Hawaii's celebrated Kona coffee, the wild and elusive nature and limited supply of beach plums adds to their appeal. Despite the best efforts of agricultural researchers, the beach plum has consistently resisted managed cultivation. Today, there are several foragers who maintain the locations of their beach plum shrubs as well-kept secrets.

Peaches

In 1895, the peach blossom was named Delaware's State Flower, almost four hundred years after Spanish explorers first brought peach trees to the Americas. The peach tree has its original roots in China, where it was described as the favorite fruit of the emperors as long ago as the tenth century. Alexander the Great first introduced peaches to Europe, and during Queen Victoria's reign, no meal was complete without a fresh peach served in a fancy napkin. By the time William Penn made his explorations of the lands that eventually became the states of Pennsylvania and Delaware, there were large stands of both peach and apple trees that had been planted by early European settlers.

During the seventeenth century, there was so much of the plentiful fresh fruit that much of it was fed to pigs and the balance distilled into brandies. These peach trees were primarily wild stock, not specially bred for any specific qualities. Isaac Reeves is considered Delaware's first commercial peach farmer. In 1832, he planted thirty acres of budded stock, and over the next ten years, he extended his orchard holdings to cover hundreds of acres. Reeves's success prompted other peach

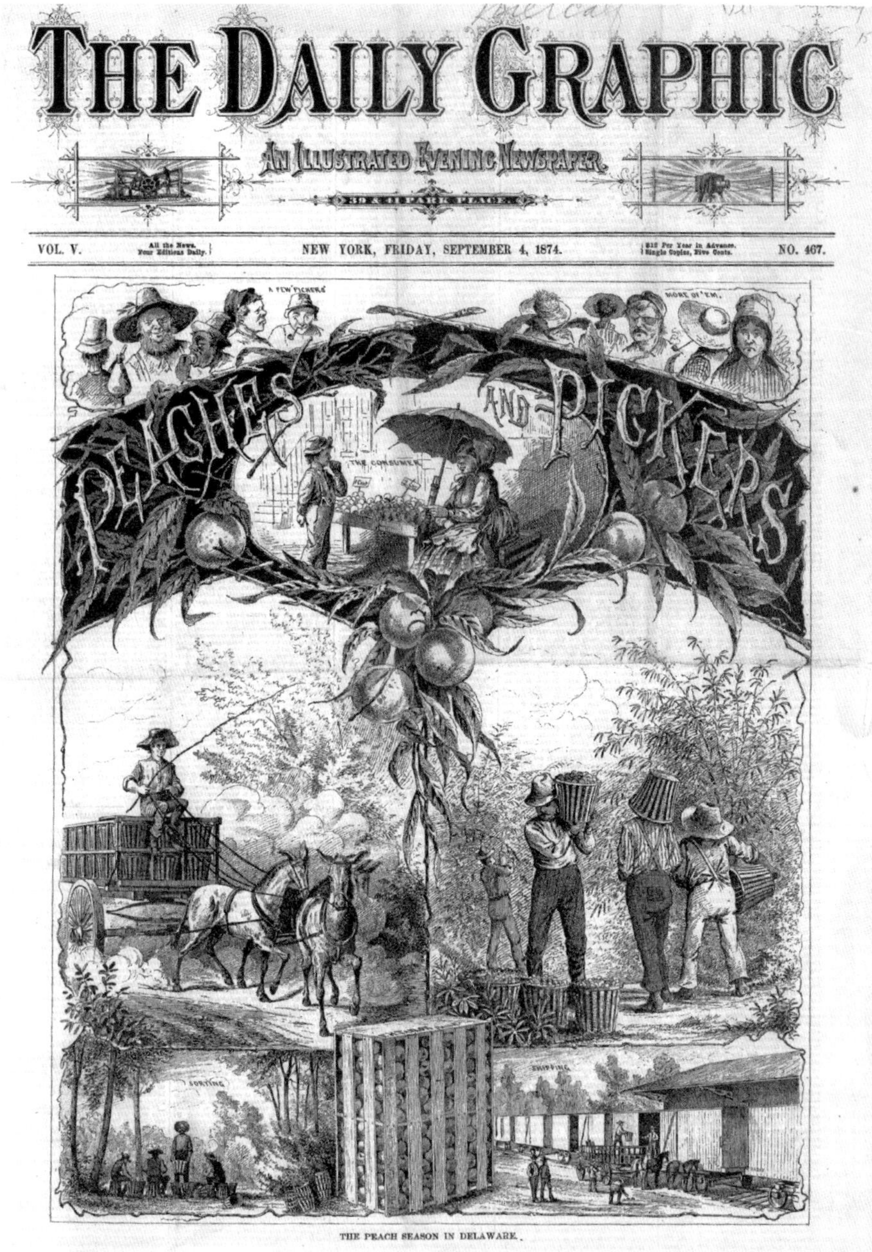

The Peach Season in Delaware, a drawing on the front page of *New York Daily Graphic*, September 4, 1874. *Courtesy of the Delaware Public Archives.*

growers to plant orchards across Southern Delaware in the hospitable soil described as "sandy loam."

As the Delaware Railroad extended its reach farther south and west across the state, peaches developed into a signature crop for Delaware. The first state in the country to commercially produce and distribute the crop, Delaware's orchards became the leading source of fruit, both fresh and preserved. Farmers typically grew several different varieties, both white and yellow fleshed, freestone (the flesh doesn't cling to the pit) and clingstone (the innermost flesh is reddish and attached to the pit). By the late eighteenth and early nineteenth centuries, property records show a number of large peach orchards located in all three counties of Delaware. These local crops were shipped by boat to Philadelphia and New York to be sold at prices as high as one dollar per bushel.

Instructions for harvesting peaches include a careful consideration of ripeness. If the crop is to be shipped, it can be picked when the peaches are still hard but ready to ripen. If the crop is to be sold locally, the fruit is left on the tree to soften a bit. Peaches intended for the cannery are selected when full and ripe but not too soft. Anything not meeting any of these criteria was no longer

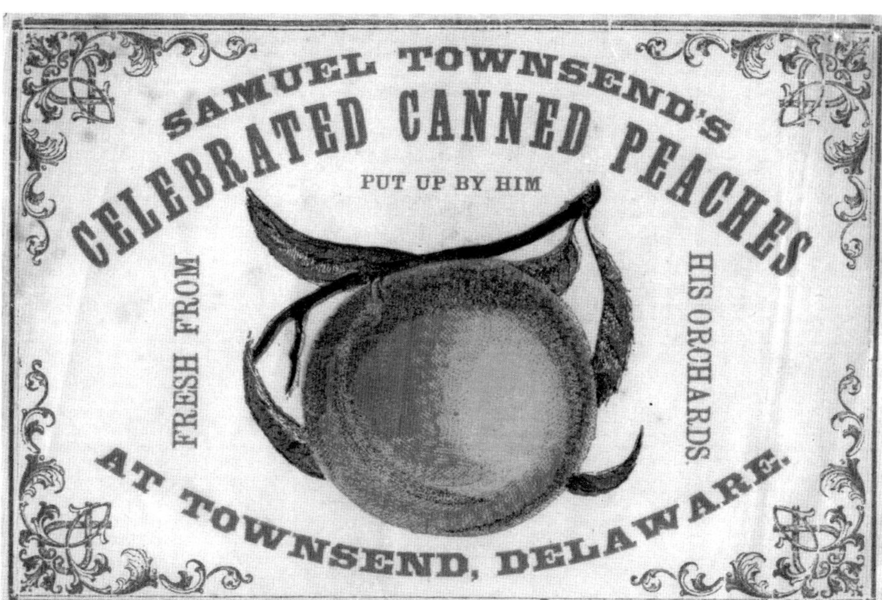

Canning label for "Samuel Townsend's Celebrated Canned Peaches, Fresh from his orchards, put up by him at Townsend, Delaware." *Courtesy of the Delaware Public Archives.*

fed to the pigs; instead, it was dried or dehydrated in a conveyor belt machine called an evaporator. Of course, some of the crop was always destined for the distillery as an important ingredient in peach brandy.

In 1867, several canneries were built in the Southern Delaware towns of Bridgeville, Laurel and Seaford, followed by one in Lewes two years later. After peaches were sorted, pitted and peeled, they were packed into tin cans, described as "cap and hole" cans. These were actually made of sheet steel covered with a thin layer of tin, to avoid a chemical reaction with the contents. The cans were filled through the opening at the top, and a metal cap was soldered in place to seal the "hole."

According to an old label in the collection of the Lewes Historical Society, the contents of some of these cans were "Choice Fresh Peaches / Hermetically Sealed by H. Hickman & Co. / Lewes, Del." There were enticements to the potential buyer: "[a] superior quality is claimed, as they were canned near the farm where they were freshly picked, well-sugared, and consequently have the natural flavor of the peach." Opening instructions did not reference a can opener, but instead, "Open the can by running a heated iron around the cap, or by placing a hot coal thereon."

In addition to canneries, another preservation method called "evaporating" became mechanized, and plants were built in towns across the region. In J. Thomas Scharf's *History of Delaware*, the author described an evaporation plant's construction in Lewes: "In 1882, William B. Yardley erected a fruit evaporating establishment near the depot. In which were placed two Williams dryers [a patented device of the time], having a capacity of 250 baskets per day."

The operation of the equipment required a two-story building with a square shaft built over a furnace in the basement. On the main floor, workers (primarily women) peeled and pitted the fruit, which was placed on wire-mesh frames. These slid into a conveyor that carried the fruit trays slowly up through the heated shaft, removing their water content.

In the year 1875, almost 6 million baskets of peaches were shipped to market from farms across Southern Delaware, more than anywhere else in the entire country. However, within twenty-five years, conditions in the peach industry would undergo a problematic change. Peach yellows, a disease fatal to the fruit tree, began to kill off the orchard stock. This widespread damage to peach crops caused some farmers to abandon the peach industry, turning instead to apples and other crops, leaving just a few successful surviving peach orchards.

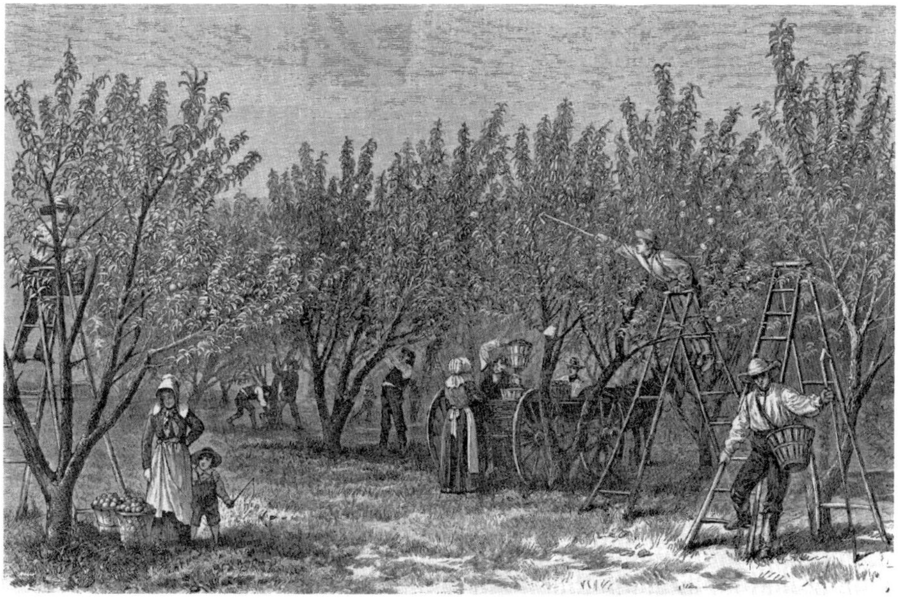

Picking Peaches in Delaware, which appeared in the September 14, 1878 edition of *Harper's Weekly*. *Courtesy of the Delaware Public Archives.*

Today, Delaware produces about 2 million pounds of peaches each year, most of which never leave the area. Some of the familiar Delaware names in today's peach-growing industry are T.S. Smith & Sons in Bridgeville, Fifer Orchards in Wyoming and Bennett Orchards in Frankford. All of these growers offer their fresh-picked peaches at on-site farm stands, as well as many of the area farmers' markets and grocery stores.

Over the course of the peach season, which runs from late June through August, a variety of peaches is available, all of which can be peeled, pitted and sliced to make Delaware's Official State Dessert: the peach pie. However, the best way to enjoy a very lovely, very ripe peach is to eat it fresh out of hand, with sticky juice running down to your elbow as you savor the succulent sweetness of a perfect Delaware peach.

APPLES

The only native apple variety found in Southern Delaware at any point in time was the crabapple, which produces a small, astringent fruit best suited for sweetened jellies or the dried fruit leather made by the Nanticokes. It was not until the arrival of European settlers, who brought seeds in the seventeenth century, that a wider array of apple varieties emerged. Because an apple tree started from seed does not grow "true" to the qualities of its parent, the seeds brought to this country from Europe produced trees that cross-pollinated with one another to create any number of new varieties.

Some of these newer breeds of apple might not have been appealing to eat fresh, but the key importance of apples rested in the production of cider, most notably the slightly alcoholic beverage we today call hard cider. Without provisions for sanitation and tools to fight bacterial contamination, drinking water could be dangerously unsafe. Cider was familiar to the Europeans, who arrived with the knowledge of cider-making. They found the apple drink both safer and healthier than water, so they started pressing apples as soon as they were ripe.

For the newly arrived settler, apple trees were among the first crops to be planted. They also considered the availability of local, native trees for cider

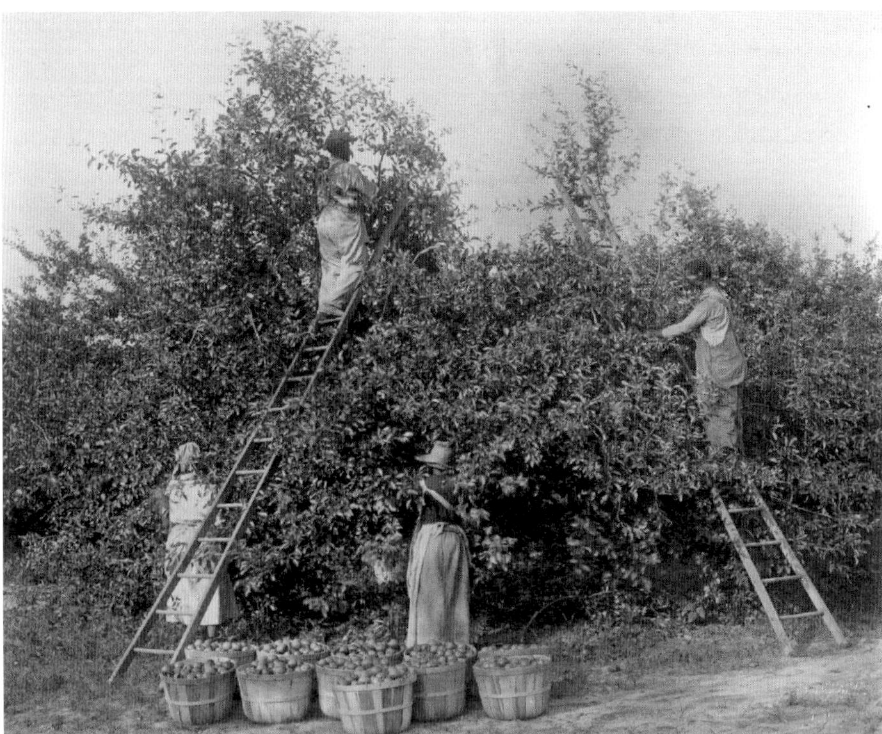

Delaware apple pickers on ladders, circa 1920. *Courtesy of the Delaware Public Archives.*

apples (eating apples fresh out of hand is a relatively modern development). In addition to the value of their juice, apples could successfully over-winter under the right conditions, making them important as food for livestock. There was no agreement on the exact process for storing an apple crop during the winter; instructions ranged from wrapping them in cloth and burying them to simply placing them in a single layer under a bedding of straw in a cool, dry place.

It seems appropriate that one of the oldest dishes made with apples was the all-American apple pie. In 1759, a recently arrived parson from Sweden, Israel Acrelius, wrote about the eating habits of his Delaware congregation and their less-than-sophisticated versions of apple pie: "Apple pie is used throughout the whole year, and when fresh Apples are no longer to be had, dried ones are used. It is the evening meal of children. House pie, in country places, is made of Apples neither peeled nor freed from their cores, and its crust is not broken if a wagon wheel goes over it."

In her 1796 cookbook, Amelia Simmons included two recipes for apple pie, as well as instructions for an apple pudding and an apple tart. Pies and

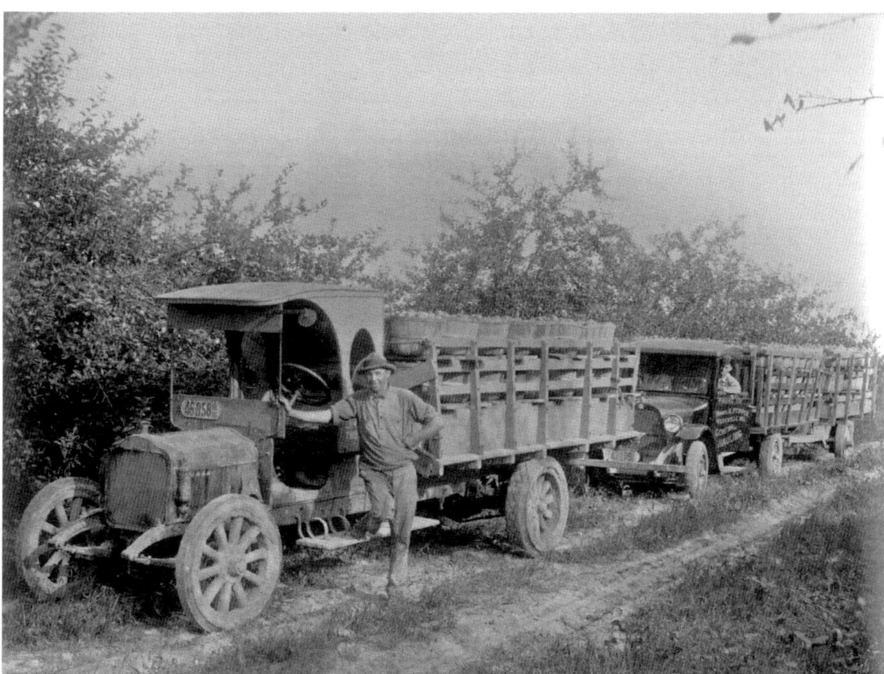

Truckers hauling baskets of apples on their way from the orchard in Sussex County, circa 1926. *Courtesy of the Delaware Public Archives.*

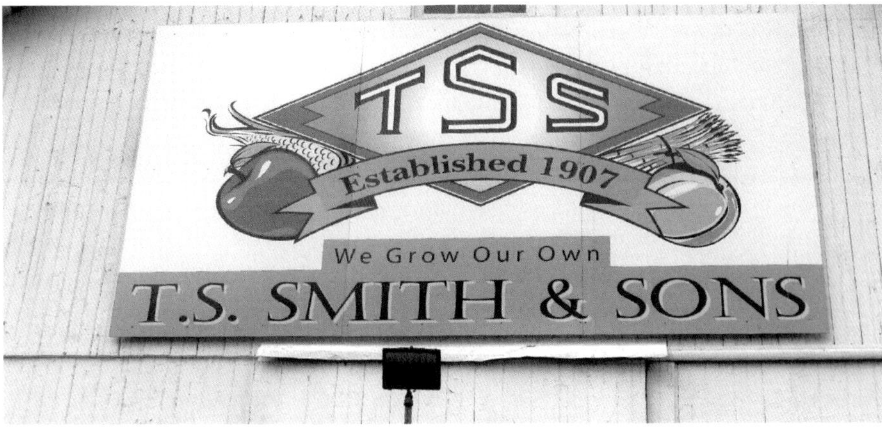

Familiar T.S. Smith & Sons sign over the entrance to its farm stand market in Bridgeville, Delaware, today. *Jack Clemons photo.*

puddings made from preserved fruit (dried or stewed) were more common in the colonial kitchen than cakes because the ingredients were more plentiful throughout the year and the oven temperature did not have to be so rigorously regulated. An apple pie served as a dessert the night before often returned to the table the following morning for breakfast, and one hopes the crust might be softer and flakier than the one described by Parson Acrelius.

When the Delaware peach crop failed in the early 1900s, many farmers turned their attention to apples. One of the earliest apple orchards in Southern Delaware was established in Bridgeville by Thomas Sterling Smith in 1907. Still in business today, the eight-hundred-acre family-owned farm is renowned for offering a dozen different apple varieties and decadent apple cider doughnuts.

Another longstanding apple producer began in 1919 with three hundred acres under the stewardship of Charles Frederick Fifer. Located just west of Dover, the fourth generation of the family now operates Fifer Orchards, where they celebrate the apple harvest with a cider festival each year.

Strawberries

Although urban legend claims that strawberries were named from the practice of protecting tender plants with a layer of straw, these berries were growing long before commercial cultivation practices developed. The almost six hundred different varieties of strawberry have evolved from wild strains, all members of the rose family. Their familiar name most likely comes from the Anglo Saxon *strea*, meaning strew or spread around, which describes their growth habit of runners straying from the plant. This may also explain why the German word for strawberries (*erdbeeren*) translates to "earth berries."

Because of its unique structure, the strawberry is actually a "false fruit"; the tiny seeds that cover the outside are the true fruit of the plant. Plump berries we find today are quite different from the original wild varieties. Forerunners of the modern strawberry hybrids were tiny, pointed gems with intense flavor. Native Americans appreciated their bright, sweet flavor and ate them both fresh and dried into fruit leathers.

European explorers returned to the continent with samples of berry plants collected in Southern Delaware and Virginia. These became quite popular both as a flowering garden plant and as a sweet fruit on the menu. Strawberries began as a commercial fruit crop with the accidental intersection of two strawberry varieties that had found their way to Europe. The Virginia strawberry, hardy native of this region, and a variety from Chile with larger berries were planted near each other and produced the ancestor of the strawberry types under cultivation today.

Successful strawberry breeding began in Europe and continued at agriculture schools and experimental stations in this country, producing strains popular with growers and consumers. Careful efforts in hybridization gave rise to important qualities such as disease resistance and improvements in flavor, color and texture. The timing of these developments coincided with the decline of the peach industry and improvements to commercial transportation throughout Southern Delaware.

From about 1870 through the 1930s, strawberries were an important cash crop, fueling the organization of strawberry auctions across the region. Immigrant and migrant laborers were essential to the growth of the strawberry industry, as the berries had to be picked by hand. Before the arrival of the railroad, these same workers helped dig canals for transport boats that carried fresh fruit to Philadelphia and New York.

In the year 1935, Delaware shipped almost 10 million quarts of strawberries. Farmers brought crates of hand-picked berries to the town center, typically located near the railroad stations, where refrigerated cars waited. The crop was tallied and payment made either in cash or tickets that served as currency with local merchants.

During this time, John G. Townsend Jr. became known as the "Strawberry King" for his successful role in the Selbyville strawberry business, which he

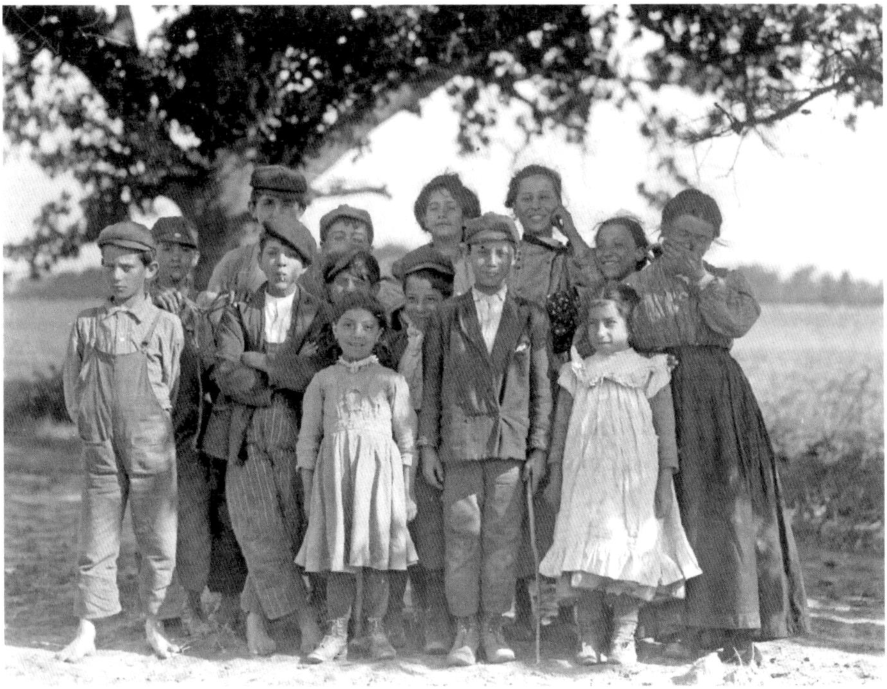

"Italian berry pickers, Giles Farm, Seaford, 1910. Ready to leave Seaford & go to Riverton, NJ to continue picking." *Courtesy of the Delaware Public Archives.*

operated as a grower, broker and processor. He planted thousands of acres of strawberries, worked as a broker to secure the best prices for his crop and operated canneries to preserve strawberries for the syrup and jam industries.

His canneries required not only a significant supply of berries but also hundreds of barrels of sugar, which severely limited the number of barrels available to other processors in the region. Some critics have described his company's operations as "hoarding the lion's share" of sugar each season, while others applauded Townsend's business acumen. To his credit, at the end of each canning season, he reportedly sold any leftover sugar to other local growers and canners at a reasonable price.

Today's strawberry crops are much smaller than during the early twentieth century. Still picked by hand, berries are brought to market by several local farms, including Magee Farms, established in 1865. Several towns hold strawberry festivals during the short summer growing season, and each year a Strawberry Queen is crowned. Because of their delicate nature, unless strawberries are eaten fresh as in a traditional shortcake, the fruit is sent to the processing plant to be frozen or transformed into jams, jellies and syrups.

WATERMELON

The well-drained, sandy soils in western Sussex County are excellent for cultivating watermelon. This area has been the site of a commercial melon industry since the mid-nineteenth century. Schooners were loaded with watermelon and traveled the Nanticoke River to Baltimore and beyond. Modern improvements to the marketing and transportation processes took several decades before the Laurel Farmers' Auction Market opened in 1940 to bring wholesale watermelon buyers and sellers together.

With an annual production of close to 100 million pounds, Delaware watermelon is now shipped to markets throughout the Atlantic seaboard, from New England to Florida. Delaware watermelons are known for their sweetness and sturdiness. The fruit ripens from mid-July through late September, and August supplies are typically the most plentiful. Because watermelon stops ripening once it's picked, Delaware watermelons are allowed to ripen on the vine to the ideal degree of sweet flavor and make their way swiftly to markets both local and remote.

One of the more recent developments in the watermelon industry is the role of recycled school buses. Formerly filled with children on their way to or from school, yellow buses are being purchased by famers and refitted to haul freshly picked watermelon from regional farms across Southern

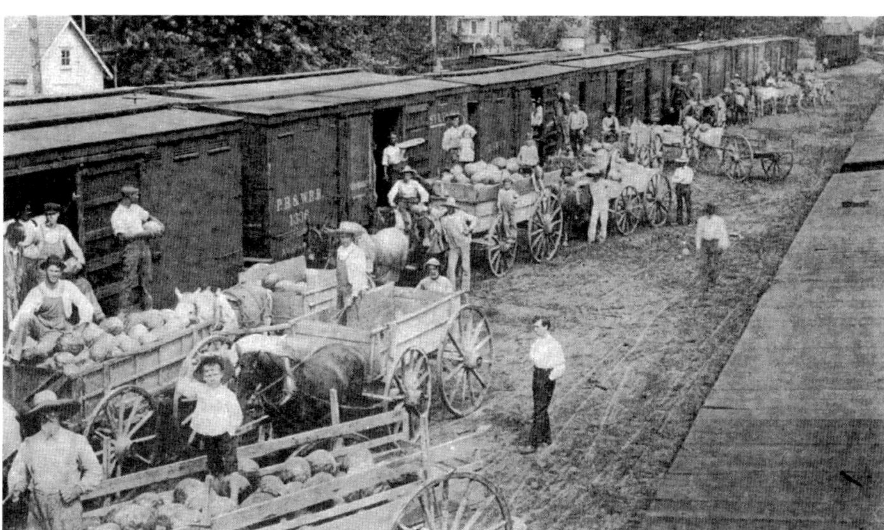

Wagons loaded with watermelons queue up at the Laurel, Delaware train station, circa 1905. *Courtesy of the Delaware Public Archives.*

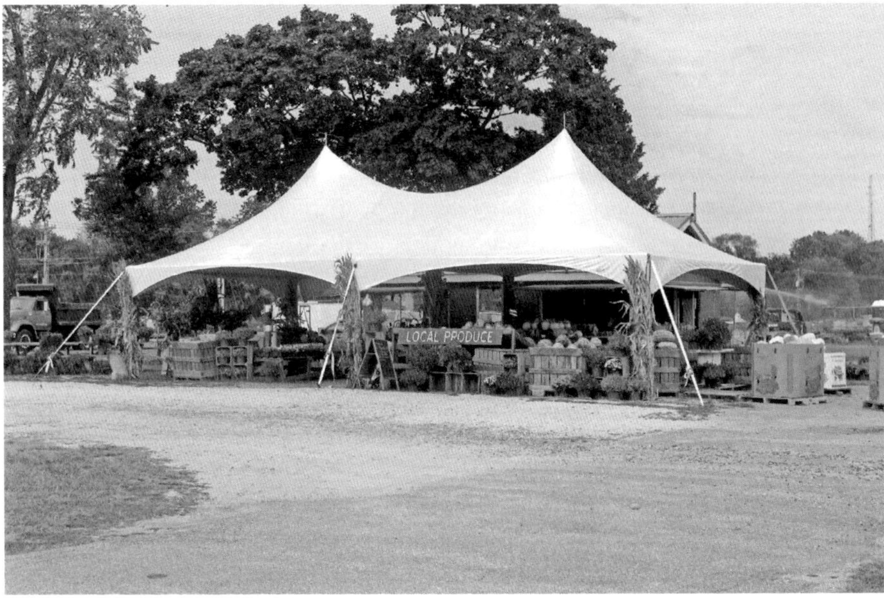

Magee's farm stand market and you-pick fields located between Nassau and Lewes, Delaware, today. *Jack Clemons photo.*

Delaware to Laurel's auction complex. Without windows, seats and most of their former tops, these forty-foot-long vehicles have become ideal watermelon trucks.

A practical evolution from the original wagons and trucks used by watermelon farmers, fruit-filled buses arrive at the Laurel Farmers' Auction, where watermelons are unloaded into shipping boxes for transport to grocery store chains in the local area, as well as to more distant markets. The best watermelons are those available at farmers' markets located on the same site as the fields filled with their vines or one of the many roadside markets.

Another fruit that is best enjoyed freshly picked at the peak of sweetness, watermelon is most commonly served in generous slices or chunks trimmed from the rind. At the same time, innovative chefs have found ways to feature watermelon on their menus in dishes such as watermelon and feta cheese salad or in creative cocktails like watermelon margaritas and watermelon martinis.

FRUIT RECIPES

Beach Plum Jelly

This recipe comes from Krista Scudlark of Backyard Jams and Jellies in Milton, Delaware. Her long experience with the challenge of balancing sugar and pectin led to this reliable combination of ingredients that delivers the signature flavor of this tart-sweet jelly.

*3½ cups beach plum juice**
6 cups sugar
2 3-ounce pouches Certo liquid pectin

Combine ingredients in a large pot and stir to combine. Bring to a simmer over medium heat and cook until the mixture begins to thicken, about 10 to 20 minutes. Pour mixture into sterilized glass jars and seal tightly.

* To collect the beach plum juice, place 2 pounds rinsed beach plums in a large pot. Cover with water and bring to a boil, mashing the plums to break open the skin and release the juice. Continue to boil for another 15 to 20 minutes, skimming off any foam that forms. Strain the mixture through a fine-mesh sieve, reserving the juice and discarding the pits.

To Preserve Peaches

Amelia Simmons provides directions on how to preserve peaches without giving any guidance on how to "clarify" sugar, an excellent example of the author assuming that the cook already knows. We now describe this as boiling sugar and water together to make simple syrup. No matter the previous steps, the brandy should be enough to preserve anything.

Put your peaches in boiling water, just give them a scald, but don't let them boil, take them out, and put them in cold water, then dry them in a sieve and put them in long wide mouthed bottles: to half a dozen peaches take a quarter of a pound of sugar, clarify it, pour it over your peaches, and fill the bottles with brandy, stop them close, and keep them in a close [dry] *place.*

Apple Pudding

This recipe from the Blue Hen's Chickens' Cook Book *sounds more like a stovetop cobbler than the puddings we see today. It was common to include either an upper or lower "paste" (pastry) baked with the pudding filling. There is much omitted here and left to the cook's experience.*

One dozen apples, peel and quarter them; two cups of pulverized sugar; season to suit with spice—use no water. For the paste:—One pound of flour, one heaping dessert-spoonful of baking powder, one cup of butter, rub in dry; three eggs. Mix with cold milk; roll out and place over the apples; cover the saucepan and cook for twenty minutes. Serve with wine or hard sauce.

Strawberry Spinach Salad

A lovely combination of flavor and textures: sweet, salty, crunchy and creamy.

2 tablespoons white wine vinegar
1 tablespoon lemon juice
⅓ cup olive oil
1 tablespoon whole grain mustard
salt and pepper, to taste
8 ounces baby spinach
½ pint strawberries
⅓ cup sliced almonds
½ cup crumbled blue cheese

Whisk together vinegar, lemon juice, olive oil and mustard; set aside. Rinse spinach, discarding broken stems and any damaged leaves. Place spinach in a serving bowl. Rinse, hull and slice the strawberries; scatter over spinach. Sprinkle almonds and cheese over spinach mixture. Drizzle with dressing and toss gently to combine.

Lattice-Top Strawberry Rhubarb Pie

This recipe comes from Debbie LaMorte, who described the pie as perfectly sweet, perfectly tart and perfectly pink.

1 pint fresh strawberries
1 pound fresh rhubarb
1¼ cups sugar
pinch of salt
3 tablespoons tapioca
1 teaspoon grated orange rind
dough for two 9-inch pies
1 tablespoon bread crumbs
4 tablespoons heavy cream
2 tablespoons butter

Preheat oven to 400 F. Wash and clean strawberries; stem the strawberries, slice in half and place in mixing bowl. Remove and discard shriveled bottoms and leaves of the rhubarb; slice ¼-inch thick and add to the strawberries. Pour in ¼ cup of sugar and sprinkle with the salt; toss gently, let mixture stand for 10 minutes and then drain. In another bowl, combine the remaining 1 cup sugar, tapioca and orange rind and toss lightly. Roll out enough dough to fit a 9-inch pie plate, line pan with dough and chill for 15 minutes. Cut remaining dough into ½-inch strips for lattice top. Remove chilled pie crust from refrigerator, dust the bottom with bread crumbs, flute the edges of the pie crust and brush edges with 2 tablespoons of the heavy cream. Combine drained strawberry-rhubarb mixture with the tapioca mixture; spoon into prepared pie shell and dot with butter. Brush the pastry strips with the remaining cream and weave strips over the top of pie into a lattice. Cover the rim of pie crust with aluminum foil to prevent scorching. Bake for 50 minutes, remove foil and bake 15 minutes longer or until crust is golden brown. Cool before serving garnished with whipped cream.

Watermelon Feta Salad

These unlikely ingredients are well-suited companions. The sweet, juicy watermelon contrasts nicely with the sharp, salty feta cheese to deliver a mouthful of flavor and texture.

1 small watermelon
2 tablespoons olive oil
1 tablespoon white Balsamic vinegar
1 tablespoon lemon juice
¼ cup mint leaves
4 ounces feta cheese
salt and pepper, to taste

Trim off watermelon rind (reserve for pickling or discard) and cut flesh into half-inch cubes, removing large seeds. In a small bowl, whisk together oil, vinegar and lemon juice. Gently toss the watermelon cubes with vinaigrette in a serving bowl. Mince mint leaves and sprinkle over salad. Add feta and stir to distribute. Season to taste with salt and pepper.

Chapter 4
ALWAYS EAT YOUR VEGETABLES

The supply of locally grown vegetables in Southern Delaware ranges from asparagus to zucchini, with a representative from almost every letter of the alphabet available for sale throughout the growing season. Much of this fresh produce is sold at farmers' markets, roadside stands and local groceries; the remainder is pickled, canned or frozen for wider distribution.

Corn

Corn is one of the truly original American crops, originating in Mexico almost seven thousand years ago. Botanically, corn is considered a grass, *Zea mays* (hence the term maize). Corn as it was originally cultivated is quite different from the tender, sweet kernels we enjoy eating today. One of the oldest types is flour corn, grown by Native Americans and also called soft or squaw corn. Several different varieties of flour corns are ground into yellow or white cornmeal and also found in blue corn tortilla chips.

The colorful bunches of what is sometimes called "Indian corn" when used in autumn decorations is technically a variety known as flint corn. These small, multicolored kernels with a tough outer shell are edible, although their taste is not at all sweet. In earlier days, flint corn was either toasted in a skillet or dried and ground (for use in puddings and pones). One familiar type of flint corn is sold today as popping corn. These have a soft, starchy center inside a very hard shell. As the kernels are heated, their internal moisture becomes steam, exploding the shell, leaving behind a white fluffy mass (delicious when salted and drowned in melted butter). All kinds of corn are capable of popping, but only this variety has enough starch to turn itself inside out with such force.

The term "field corn" (as opposed to "table corn") usually refers to dent corn, the most widely grown variety and found in everything from cornflakes to biodegradable plastics to ethanol. Almost all the field corn grown in Southern Delaware goes to the poultry industry as chicken feed. Softer than Indian corn but harder than flour corn, these kernels have a thick case around a starchy center. The name comes from its appearance: as the inside dries and shrinks, the outside shell develops a dent.

The corn we look forward to eating off the cob every summer is sweet corn. These include the popular hybridized, sugar-enhanced varieties like Supersweet that contain up to 10 percent sugar, compared to field corn's mere 4 percent. Although these varieties have been bred to retain their flavor and moisture for a longer time after harvest, purists will insist that sweet corn should be eaten the very same day it is picked. Sweet corn will convert almost

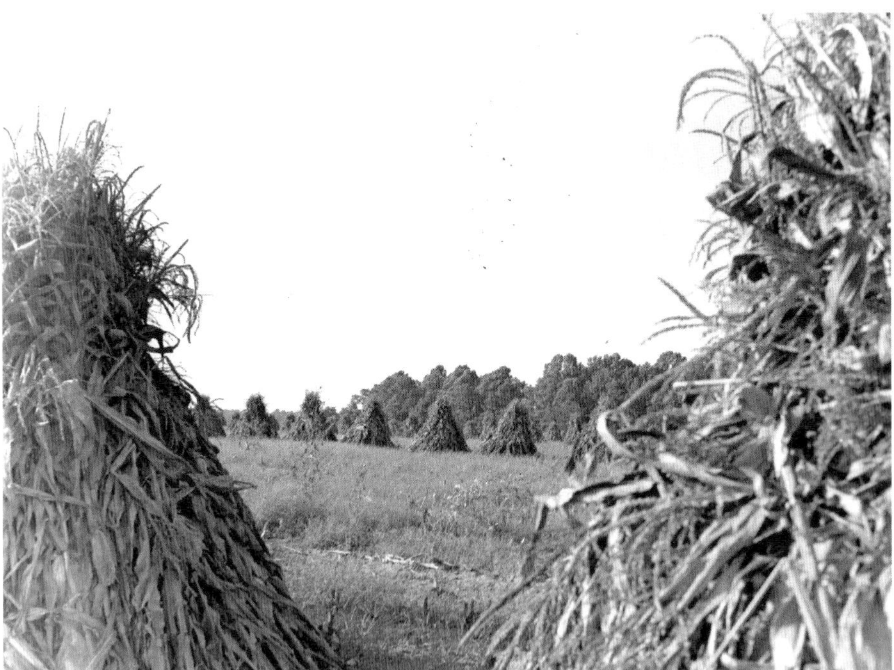

Cornstalks bundled into cones and left on the fields to dry before becoming animal feed and bedding. *Courtesy of the Delaware Public Archives.*

half its sugar to starch within twenty-four hours, so if you can't cook it the same day, be sure to store it in the refrigerator to minimize any loss.

Corn has long been known as one of the "three sisters" (corn, squash and beans) cultivated by the Native Americans and has been a staple food for centuries. For the Nanticokes, corn was harvested by plucking cobs off the cornstalks by hand. The husks were stripped with a leather loop, and then the cobs were stored in open cribs to dry. To remove the hard kernels from the cob, the ears were either rubbed against one another or threaded through a hollow log fitted with a grate, which allowed the kernels to fall into a vessel waiting below. The next step was to remove the tough exterior shells from the kernels by soaking them in a solution of wood ash. The soaking process chemically changed the nature of the corn, allowing it to form a rough dough when mixed with water.

Once the plump, white inner flesh of the corn kernels (called hominy) was thoroughly rinsed, it was ready to eat, usually boiled into a stew with meat or

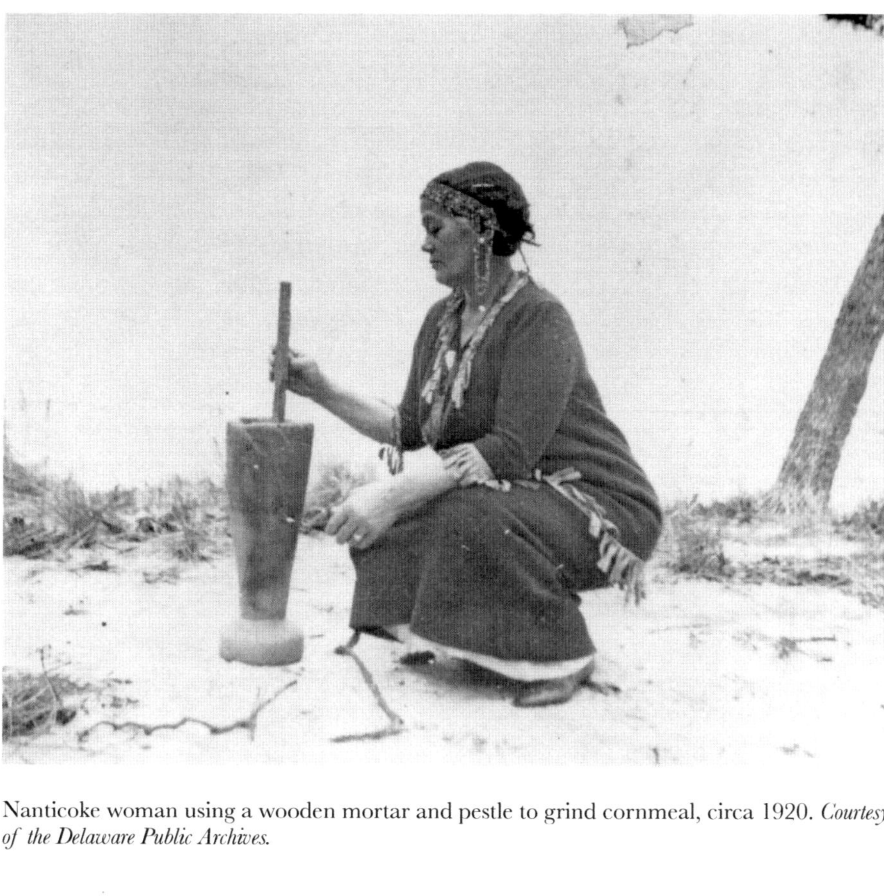

Nanticoke woman using a wooden mortar and pestle to grind cornmeal, circa 1920. *Courtesy of the Delaware Public Archives.*

fish. Alternatively, the hominy was dried and then ground in a large mortar and pestle made of wood. This process was repeated several times, scooping up the grits and pouring them back into the mortar, until the desired size of the cornmeal was reached.

Now the cornmeal could be cooked into a variety of dishes, including ash cake and johnnycake. The first was made from a disk of corn dough wrapped in basswood leaves and set in the guttering embers of a fire to cook. Another slow-cooking dish was cornmeal porridge, which was stirred regularly as it simmered overnight. For johnnycakes, a type of cornmeal pancake, cornmeal and water were mixed into a somewhat runny batter. To cook the cakes, a half cup was poured onto a wooden paddle and held at an angle toward the open fire to brown. Corn pone is the likely ancestor of our modern corn bread: cornmeal mixed into a thickened mush and baked in the oven into a dense loaf.

From the first farmers through today, fresh corn on the cob was eagerly sought as soon as the early harvest became available. These days, farm stands and markets post signs on their bins proclaiming "just picked." Cooks and connoisseurs seek out silky tassels and still-damp husks that signal they will find tender, juicy kernels within. Corn is eaten directly from the cob, preserved through canning or freezing and incorporated into signature dishes such as corn and crab chowder.

Corn feeds the families of Southern Delaware in multiple ways. Fresh corn (and later frozen and canned options) has been on the local menu for centuries. Each household has a special corn chowder recipe, incorporating bacon, potato, crabmeat and other (usually secret) flavorful ingredients. In addition to the varieties of corn eaten in its fresh or preserved forms, field corn feeds the massive inventory managed by poultry farmers, who in turn feed us with their tender broiler chickens.

LIMA BEANS

Pole lima beans were the likely variety of limas originally cultivated by the Nanticokes. As one of the "three sisters," the lima bean vine relied on the cornstalk as a trellis around which it wound as it grew, flowered and developed pods filled with beans. Also described as a "corn hill" bean, the beans of the pole lima are larger, and the plant is more temperamental to manage than the baby lima bean varieties grown widely in the region today.

Throughout Southern Delaware, you will still find small-scale farmers or backyard gardeners growing patches of pole lima beans for their own tables and some local markets. Pole beans have been served to Delaware families for centuries and can often be found for sale at seasonal farmers' markets. These sport a variety of color variations—for example, the Christmas Pole Lima, which is speckled red and white, quite unlike the traditional green Fordhook lima bean.

The other type of lima bean you will find planted across large tracts of farmland is known as the baby lima bean for its smallish size. These have been raised commercially for canneries and, subsequently, the frozen vegetable industry since the mid-nineteenth century. During the Second World War, demand for preserved foods was greater than there were workers to handle the processing jobs, causing some prominent canneries to close their doors.

Today, Delaware grows more acres of lima beans than any other state in the country. One reason is the climate enjoyed by farms situated along the Delaware Bay. Here you will find the combination of high humidity and mild temperatures optimal for the lima bean plants. A system of contract farming has been in place for lima beans since the 1880s. Before the crops are planted each season, a farmer negotiates with a processor to deliver a specific quantity at an agreed-on price. Although many of these arrangements in the past were made with Delaware canneries, more of today's lima bean crops are destined for the vegetable freezing plants still operating in the state.

Driving along the back roads that crisscross Southern Delaware during the late summer, visitors may have the opportunity to watch a lima bean harvester crawl through the fields, stripping pods from the vines on their way to the processing plants to be shelled, graded and flash-frozen for sale under familiar brands such as PictSweet, Hanover Foods and Seabrook. Locals will assert that nothing is as tender and tasty as fresh lima beans. Forget about the mushy mess served in high school cafeterias; fresh lima beans are firm and flavorful, especially when mixed with corn kernels to make a batch of a local favorite: succotash.

Potatoes

Potatoes have had an interesting journey becoming such a popular food in this country. White and sweet potatoes both originated in the Andes. The golden-orange sweet potato traveled north into the United States from South America along with Spanish explorers. White potatoes found their way to Europe in the returning ships of English explorers. Initially, only sweet potatoes were cultivated as a food crop until Irish immigrants brought white potatoes when they came to the American colonies.

Sweet potatoes have long been a crop grown on local farms, originally only in sufficient quantity to feed members of the farmer's family. In the nineteenth century, as other crops were shipped to consumers beyond the borders of Delaware, brokers recognized that the mild climate and fertile soil of Southern Delaware combined to produce a sweet potato that reportedly tasted better than those grown in Carolina or Texas.

Starting from the mid-1800s, this became an extremely profitable commercial crop for the farmers of the region. The towns of Seaford and Laurel were the epicenters of sweet potato production, the profits from which made many farmers quite wealthy. However, like the stories of changing fortunes associated with several other food crops, Sussex County sweet potatoes became dominant in the market, with supplies exceeding 1 million bushels in 1924, until a blight known as black rot essentially obliterated the crop in 1940.

A small reminder of the sweet potato crops that were so prevalent in the past century is the inventory of potato houses scattered across the region. The sole purpose of these two-story (and sometimes three-story) buildings was to hold the sweet potatoes at a constant temperature (about fifty degrees) for several weeks following their harvest. This entailed running a coal stove during the coldest of the winter days to cure the delicate potato. The curing process allowed the skin to heal cuts or nicks they suffered during harvest before the potatoes could be safely stored for long periods of time.

Today, both sweet and white potatoes sold by local farmers are found in much smaller supply than the volumes sold in the 1920s, yet their texture and flavor continue to please consumers. From purple fingerlings to ruddy sweets, the potato has not gone out of favor.

TOMATOES

Whether you consider the tomato a fruit or a vegetable, this juicy red orb remains a key ingredient for both the cuisine and commerce of Southern Delaware.

To first address the classification question, the tomato itself is botanically considered the fruit of the plant because it is the edible, fleshy material covering its seeds. However, it is treated as a vegetable for agricultural purposes because of the way the plants are grown for food. So, technically, they are either or both. Legally, the tomato is classified as a vegetable, based on an 1893 Supreme Court ruling to clarify import taxes (importers were claiming it was a fruit to avoid being taxed).

In culinary terms, tomatoes perform beautifully in both sweet dishes (as fruit does) and savory preparations (similar to vegetables) despite having to overcome an unfavorable reputation. The botanical name for the tomato, *lycopersicon*, translates to "wolf peach," or poison in a pretty package. As a member of the nightshade family (along with potatoes, eggplant and several poisonous plants), the tomato's reputation was tarnished by association. Tomatoes were avoided as a food across Europe and by European immigrants to this country.

There may be a grain of truth in the possibility of being poisoned from eating tomatoes: highly acidic tomato juices could interact with elements used to make pewter plates and dishes used in the sixteenth century, potentially leaching lead from the metal and sickening the tomato-eater.

Another possibility for why the tomato was shunned, despite its documented place in Thomas Jefferson's gardens, was its reputation as an aphrodisiac. Early settlers looking for religious freedom and purity might have been confused by the Italian name for tomato, *pomme de Maure*, or "apple of the Moors," earning this name because tomatoes arrived in Europe as an import from the Spanish (sometimes called Moors). Spoken aloud, the name sounds close to the French phrase *pomme d'amour*, or "apple of love."

None of the earliest cookbooks makes any mention of tomatoes as an ingredient until Mary Randolph described how to stew them in her *Virginia Housewife* of 1860. By that time, farmers in Southern Delaware had learned how ideally suited tomatoes were to the canning and bottling process. Because of the acidic nature of the tomato and its ease of processing (no hard shell or pod to remove), the crop could be swiftly picked and sent to the cannery.

According to the 1919 *Directory of Canners in the United States*, more than one hundred firms operated across Delaware, most of them in the southern

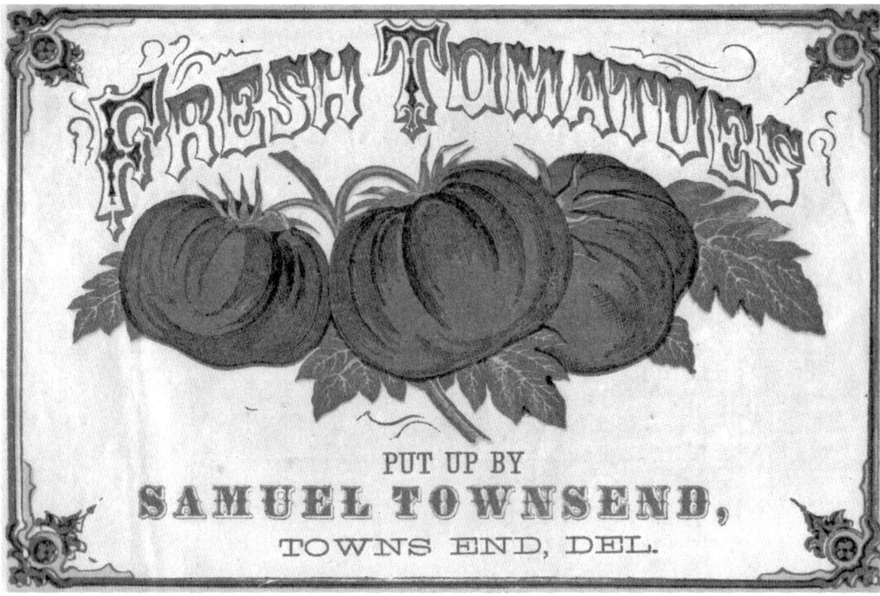

Canning label for "Fresh Tomatoes put up by Samuel Townsend, Towns End, Delaware." *Courtesy of the Delaware Public Archives.*

regions of the state. By this time, tomatoes had changed from an undesirable food to one that was celebrated for its nutritional advantages. Canneries produced a consistent array of tomato products for the home pantry, including soups, sauces, ketchups, tomato paste and peeled tomatoes.

While the region experienced a decline in the tomato processing business later in the twentieth century, the tomato remains an extremely popular food in its freshest form through the summer months. Many small, local farmers have successfully reintroduced colorful heirloom varieties of tomatoes. Instead of the standard red beefsteak, you can find yellow, orange and variegated tomatoes in all sorts of not-quite-round shapes. From as tiny as grapes to the size of a small melon, the freshly picked tomato is the star of the summer table.

VEGETABLE RECIPES

Baked Corn Pone

This is similar to the technique used by the Nanticokes when they cooked cornmeal mush wrapped in leaves overnight in the remains of a fire. Early settlers made their adjustments to this recipe, filling a large cast-iron cauldron to cook the pone in the hearth at the heart of the house. This comes from The First State: First Lady's Recipe Book *and reflects an important modern convenience in today's kitchens: the oven.*

1 tablespoon butter
1 tablespoon bacon grease
2½ pounds cornmeal
2 tablespoons salt
2 to 3 quarts boiling water
1 cup dark brown sugar
⅓ cup molasses
1 cup flour

Preheat oven to 250 F. Generously grease the inside of a large Dutch oven with butter and bacon grease; set aside. Combine the cornmeal and salt in a very large mixing bowl. Pour 2 quarts of boiling water into the bowl and stir. Add more water, if necessary, to reach the consistency of a thick muffin batter. Stir in brown sugar, molasses and flour. Transfer dough to the prepared pot and place it in the oven, uncovered. Check after 2 hours and cover the pot when a nice crust has formed. Continue baking until cooked through, about 1 additional hour. To serve, cut slices of the corn pone and fry in melted butter.

Corn Chowder

Hints of smoky bacon and onion, sweet corn and fresh crabmeat combine in a satisfying bowl of rich flavor and texture.

4 ears of corn on the cob
2 slices bacon

1 chopped celery stalk
1 chopped onion
1 tablespoon flour
1 potato, peeled and diced
½ cup diced red bell pepper
2 cups corn broth
2 scallions, sliced
1½ cups cream
2 cups fresh crab meat
salt and pepper, to taste
1 tablespoon snipped chives

Shuck the corn and collect the kernels in a bowl; set aside. Break the cobs in half and place them in a saucepan with enough water to cover. Bring to a boil; cover the pot, reduce heat and simmer for 15 minutes. Meanwhile, in a medium saucepan, sauté the chopped bacon until crisp. Remove the bacon with a slotted spoon and reserve for another use. Add celery and onion to the pot and sauté until softened, about 5 minutes. Sprinkle flour over vegetables and cook, stirring constantly until flour turns golden. Add potato, red bell pepper and 2 cups of corn broth, scraping up and dissolving flour completely. Simmer, stirring often until potatoes are tender, about 15 minutes. Add scallions, reserved corn kernels, cream and two-thirds of the crab meat. Simmer until heated through, about 5 minutes. Adjust seasonings and serve garnished with chives and generous dollops of reserved crab meat. Yield: 4 servings.

Succotash

The name of this dish comes from the Native American word misickquatosh, a mixture of corn and kidney beans cooked in bear grease. A key to this dish is the inclusion of the milky liquid from fresh corncobs.

1 cup fresh lima beans
pinch salt
3 ears corn on the cob

1 tablespoon butter
1 minced shallot
salt and white pepper, to taste

Place the lima beans in a saucepan with just enough water to cover. Add salt and bring to a boil over medium high. Reduce heat and gently simmer until beans are firm-tender, about 5 minutes; do not overcook. Drain and set aside. Shuck the corn; discard husks. On a rimmed cutting board, slice the kernels from the cobs, reserving all the milky juice. When cobs are stripped, grasp the stem end with one hand and tightly wrap the other hand around the tip of the ear. Pressing firmly, slide your hand down the ear, squeezing out and collecting any remaining juice; discard cobs. Melt butter in a medium saucepan; add shallot and sauté until soft, about 3 minutes. Add lima beans, corn and corn liquid; simmer on low until heated through, about 5 minutes. Season to taste with salt and white pepper. Yield: 4 servings.

Sweet Green Tomato Pickles

Courtesy of Ivy Hail Bennett's recipe collection from the early 1900s, this dish provides a destination for those green tomatoes that were picked too soon to send to the cannery.

1 peck green tomatoes, sliced
6 large onions, sliced
1 cup salt
2 quarts water
1 quart white vinegar
4 quarts apple cider vinegar
1 quart brown sugar
½ pound ground mustard
1 tablespoon cloves
2 tablespoons cinnamon
2 tablespoons ginger

Toss together tomatoes, onion and salt in a large bowl. Cover with plastic wrap and let stand overnight. The next morning, drain off any juices and place the tomatoes and onion in a large pot. Add 2 quarts water and 1 quart white vinegar. Bring to a boil and simmer for 5 minutes. Drain and apportion vegetables into canning jars about halfway full; set aside. In a large pot, combine remaining ingredients. Bring to a boil and simmer for 15 minutes. Pour pickling liquid into the jars and seal.

Caprese Salad

This traditional Italian appetizer deserves your perfectly ripe tomatoes, as seen in the color photo.

2 large ripe tomatoes
8 ounces fresh mozzarella cheese
16 fresh basil leaves
salt and pepper, to taste
2 tablespoons olive oil
2 tablespoons Balsamic vinegar

Slice tomatoes and cheese. Arrange them overlapping on a serving plate, tucking a basil leaf between the slices. Season to taste with salt and pepper. Drizzle with olive oil and Balsamic vinegar. Yield: 4 servings.

Chapter 5

GRAINS AND GRISTMILLS

Grains or cereal grains, are named for Ceres, an ancient Roman goddess of agriculture. Grains are considered any plant from the botanical grass family that yields an edible seed. Because they provide an inexpensive source of nutrition—readily available protein and high percentage of carbohydrates—grains have been harvested across the globe for centuries.

MILLS

Flour was an essential ingredient in the Southern Delaware diet. Wheat was grown on family farms from the time the first settlers established themselves in the area. In the earliest days, transforming the grist or grain into flour was a labor-intensive process entailing a crude mortar and pestle made of wood or a pair of flat stones called a quern that ground the grain between the two hard surfaces. However, an extensive network of rivers, streams and inlets in the region readily supported the proliferation of water-powered mills.

By the early eighteenth century, gristmills and sawmills had been built throughout the area, sited where dams had been constructed to harness the energy of streams and rivers. Initially, farmers brought their wheat crops to the mills and paid for the milling service with a portion of the resulting flour. Since overland travel was arduous, mills were found within five or ten miles of nearby farmsteads so the farmer's trip to the mill could be completed in

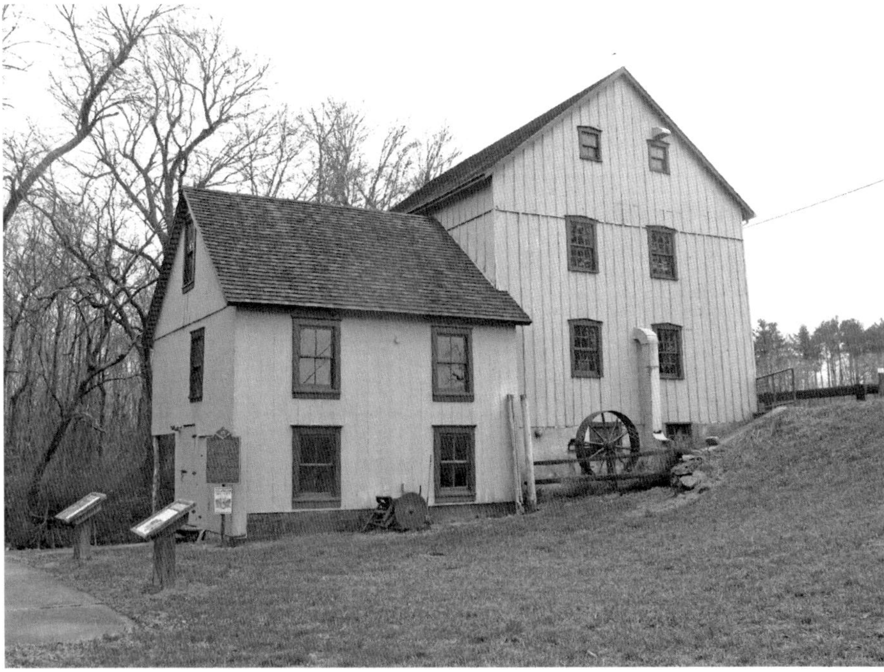

Abbott's Mill as it appears today; the historical site offers educational programs on the development of gristmills and sawmills. *Jack Clemons photo.*

a single day. Town centers clustered near the waterside mill sites, which also became the distribution center for goods traveling by boat.

Abbott's Mill, located in Milford, provides an example of how important mills were to the surrounding farmers. Shortly after its construction, the mill's owner, Nathan Wiley, along with several of his neighbors, presented a petition to the Court of General Sessions in April 1802. They claimed that the mill had been built at great cost to meet the needs of the local families. They successfully lobbied for the construction of a road extension leading to the location of the new mill.

One clever Delaware inventor is credited with drastically improving milling operations. In the late 1700s, Oliver Evans of Newport, Delaware, designed a series of automated bucket elevators and conveyors that transformed milling from a labor-intensive process into a one-person job. A rolling screen sifted dirt from the incoming grain, which was carried up in buckets to be ground and then down through chutes to be cooled. Previously, the freshly ground flour, hot and damp from the mill stones, was spread on the floor and stirred with a rake to keep it from caking, a rather unsanitary approach. Evans developed a device to mechanically rake the flour within an enclosed bin before it was sent through the hopper to be bagged or packed into barrels.

Since this mechanization was developed before the United States had a patent office, many millers began adopting his design without first securing permission, including an employee working at Thomas Jefferson's plantation. In 1790, the third patent from the newly formed department was issued to Oliver Evans for his invention. Almost thirty years later, Evans received a check from President Jefferson, drawn on the bank of the United States (not a personal account), as payment for the use of Evans's design.

The milling history of Southern Delaware remains evident in current town names, such as Milford, Millsboro and Millville. Although the structures are gone, many ponds carried the name of their mills: Betts Mill Pond, Red Mill Pond and Cubbage Mill Pond. Almost every stream and river branch provided energy to operate a mill and offer access to water transportation. These were often called a "landing" in many place names, among them New Wharf Landing, Red House Landing and Holts Landing. The only exception to the mill influence in "mil" names is found in Milton, an early shipbuilding town that had a mill on the Broadkill River, but residents insist that it was actually named for the poet John Milton.

Grain crops emerged as important for both table and trade in the early nineteenth century and continue through today, specifically wheat, barley, oats and rye.

WHEAT

While bread was eaten at almost every meal, it did not resemble the soft, white bread found in supermarkets today. The earliest breads were the corn pones and dense whole-grain breads cooked in the hearth fires of colonial-era homes. As the first wheat crops became available, flour made it possible to bake a greater variety of breads and rolls.

One of the key grains to become a significant cash crop in Southern Delaware during the eighteenth century was soft red winter wheat. Able to withstand more humidity than other varieties, it was ideally suited to the growing conditions and generally mild winters in Southern Delaware. Many farmers grew corn in the summer and wheat in the winter, capitalizing on the complementary timing to make the best use of their lands.

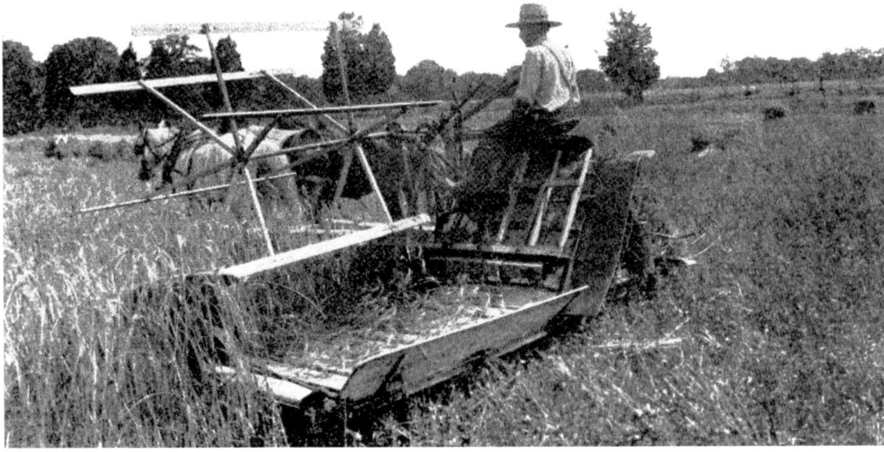

A team of horses pulls this harvester through wheat fields in Frederika, "Kent County's second largest crop." *Courtesy of the Delaware Public Archives.*

Soft red winter wheat has less gluten-forming protein and more carbohydrates than other types of winter or summer wheats. It is best for baked goods that do not require kneading and produces a tender texture in foods such as cakes, biscuits, pancakes and pastries. Hard wheats have more gluten, which gives dough mixed from them greater elasticity, which is preferable in bread-making.

Before the invention of fast-acting leavening agents (baking powder and baking soda), yeast was the only ingredient that made dough rise. It wasn't sold in foil packets but rather found naturally in the environment as strains of wild yeast a baker collected from what floated on the nearby breezes. To start, a combination of flour and water was set on a window ledge or other protected area open to the outside air. Yeast landed and began the job of leavening.

The initial fermentation could take a week or more as the yeast ate the flour, creating a food source for naturally occurring lactic bacteria. They, in turn, create an acidic environment tolerable only to the yeast (and none of the other microorganisms). This gave the dough a sharp flavor (sourdough), as well as encouraged the proliferation of more yeast, creating generous amounts of carbon dioxide and ethanol to leaven the dough. This teeming culture could persist for years, if properly fed and stored. Each time some of

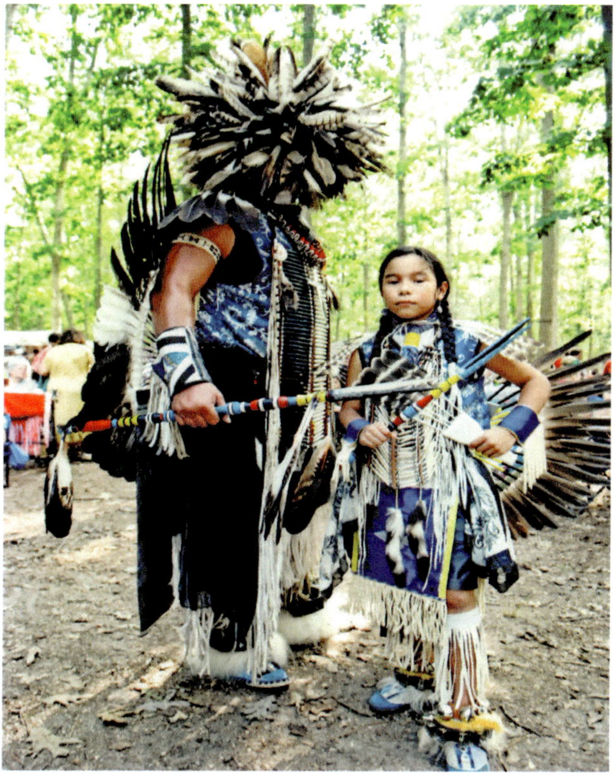

Charles Eagle Tail and son at the Nanticoke Powwow in September 2011. *Courtesy of Bob Spross, Georgetown, Delaware.*

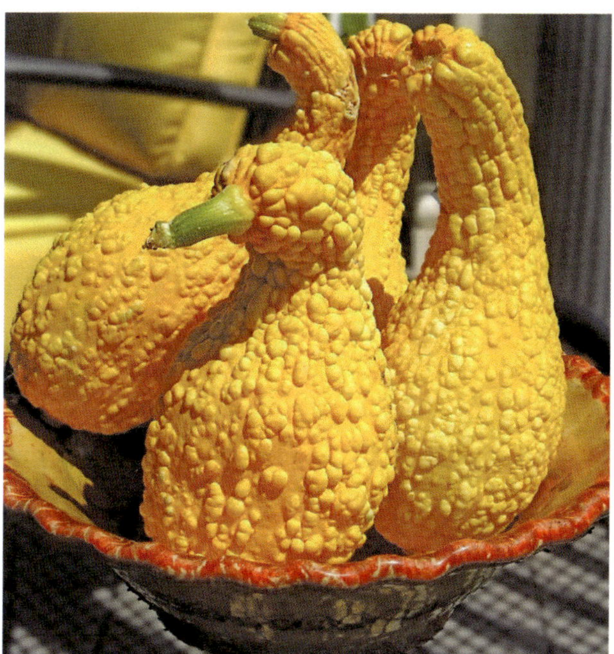

Summer squash, one of the trio of plants called the "three sisters," grown together for mutual benefit by the Nanticoke natives. *Jack Clemons photo.*

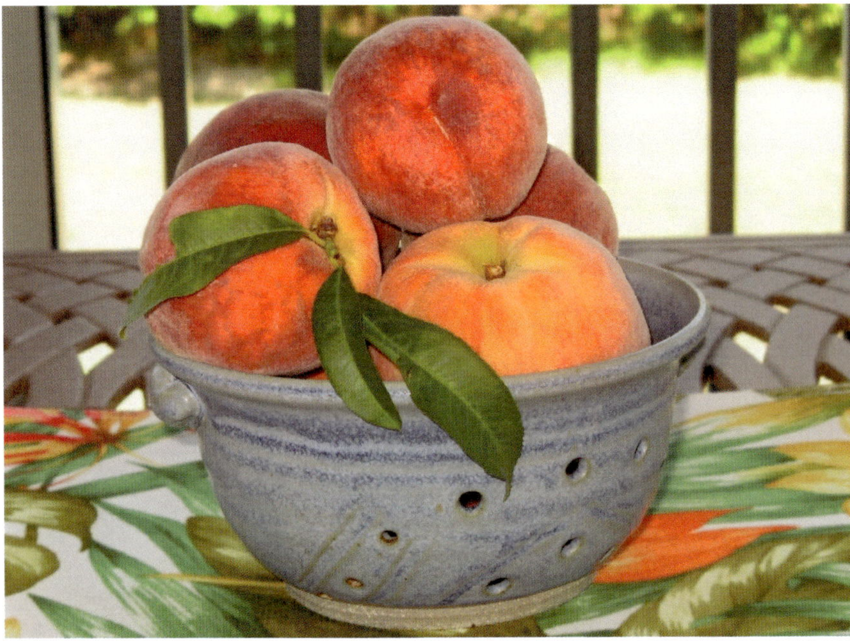

Delaware peaches have returned to the region after "peach yellows" destroyed the orchards at the end of the nineteenth century. *Jack Clemons photo.*

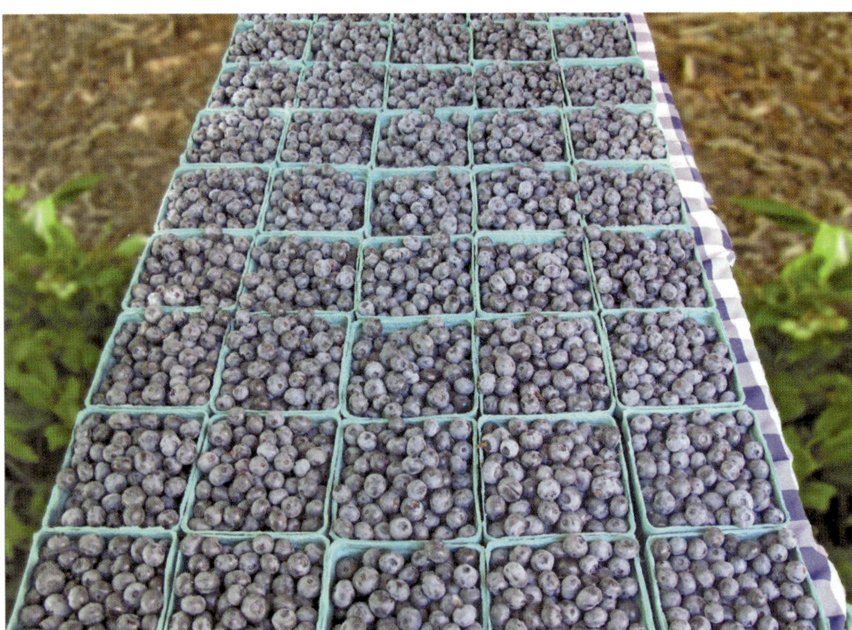

Flats of blueberries from Bennett Orchards offered for sale at the Lewes Farmers' Market in 2015. *Jack Clemons photo.*

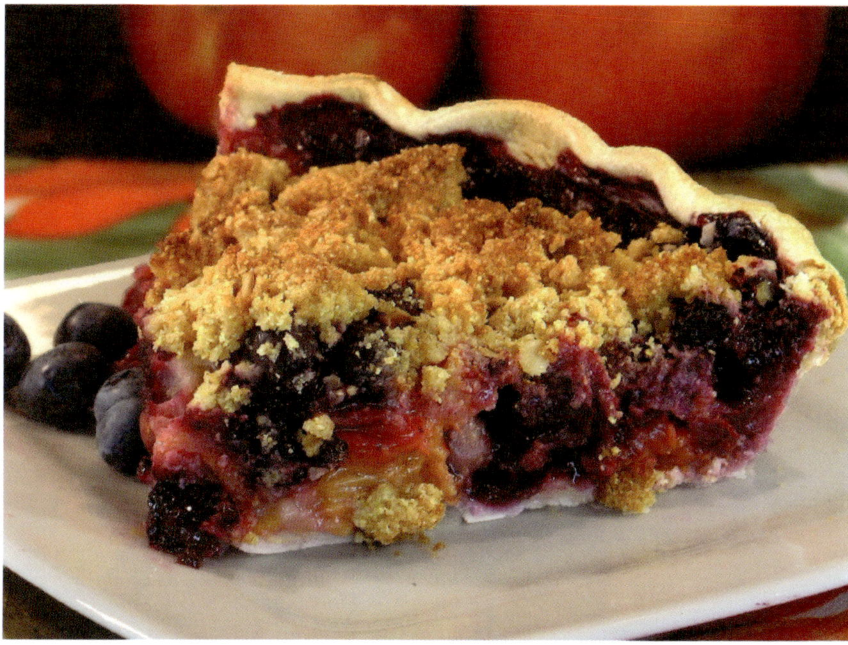

Crumb-Top Peach Blueberry Pie combines two of Southern Delaware's signature fruits. *Jack Clemons photo.*

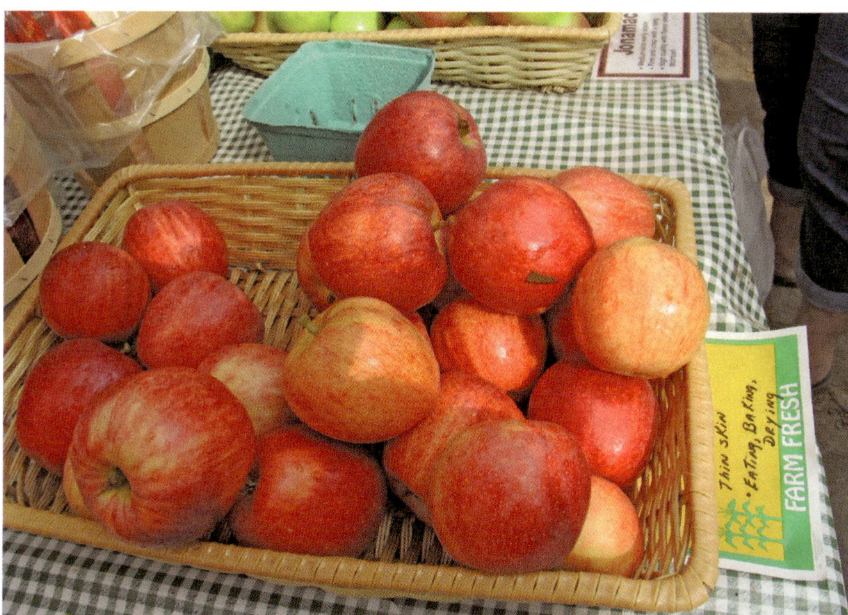

Delaware apples were important to European settlers for use in cider-making. Today, fruit is harvested for commercial markets and retail consumers. *Jack Clemons photo.*

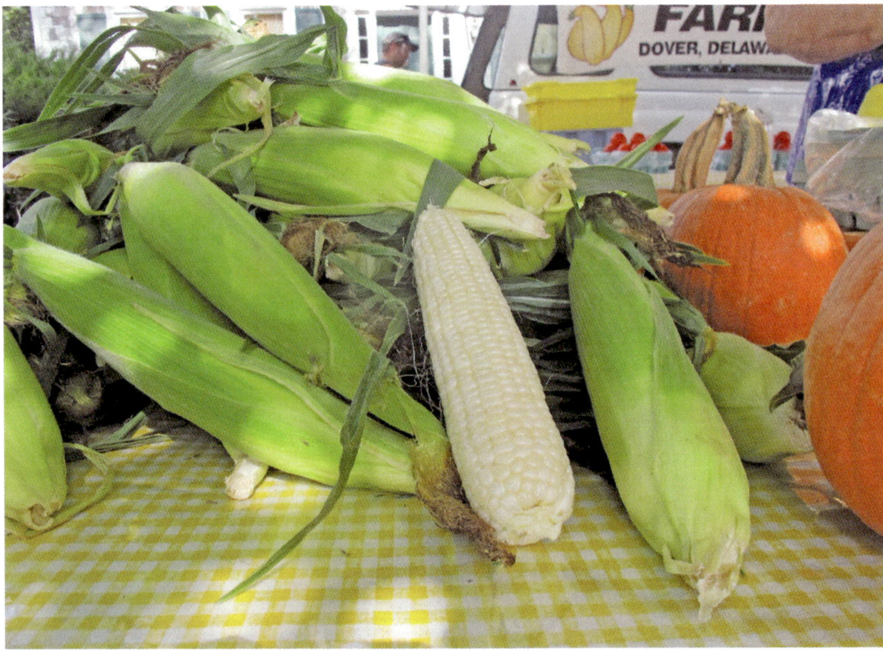

Fresh white corn at the Rehoboth Beach Farmers' Market in 2015. *Jack Clemons photo.*

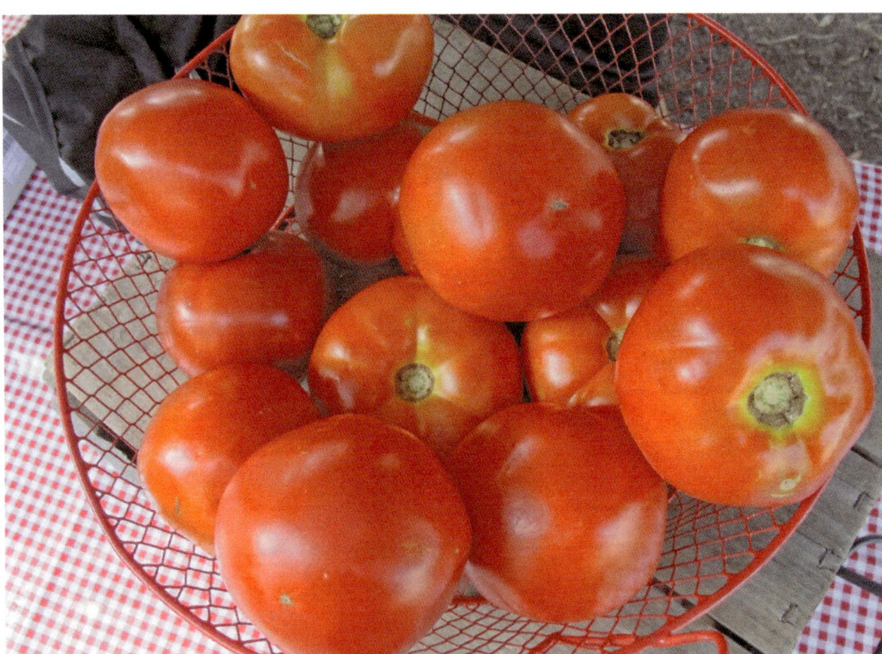

A basket of vine-ripe Delaware tomatoes in 2015. *Jack Clemons photo.*

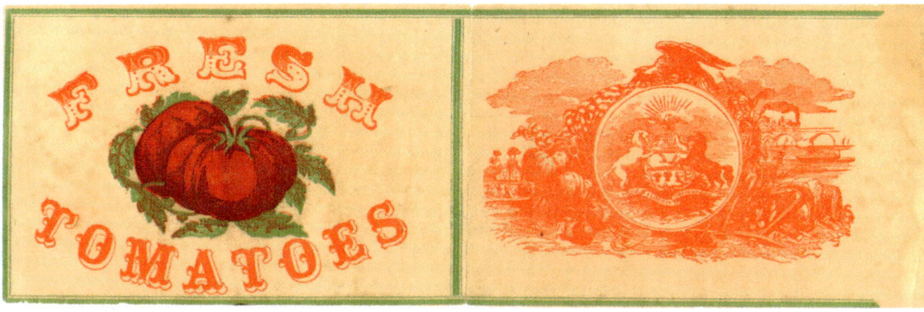

Tomato canning label with stylized farm implements, crops, ships, American eagle and horses. "Virtue Liberty Independence." *Courtesy of the Delaware Public Archives.*

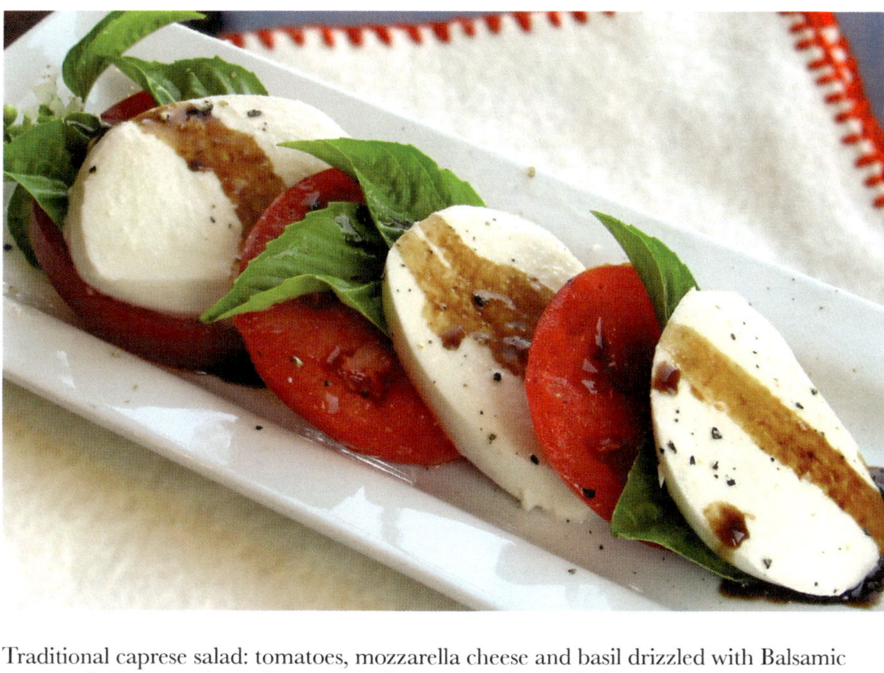

Traditional caprese salad: tomatoes, mozzarella cheese and basil drizzled with Balsamic vinegar. Collect your ingredients at the farmers' market. *Jack Clemons photo.*

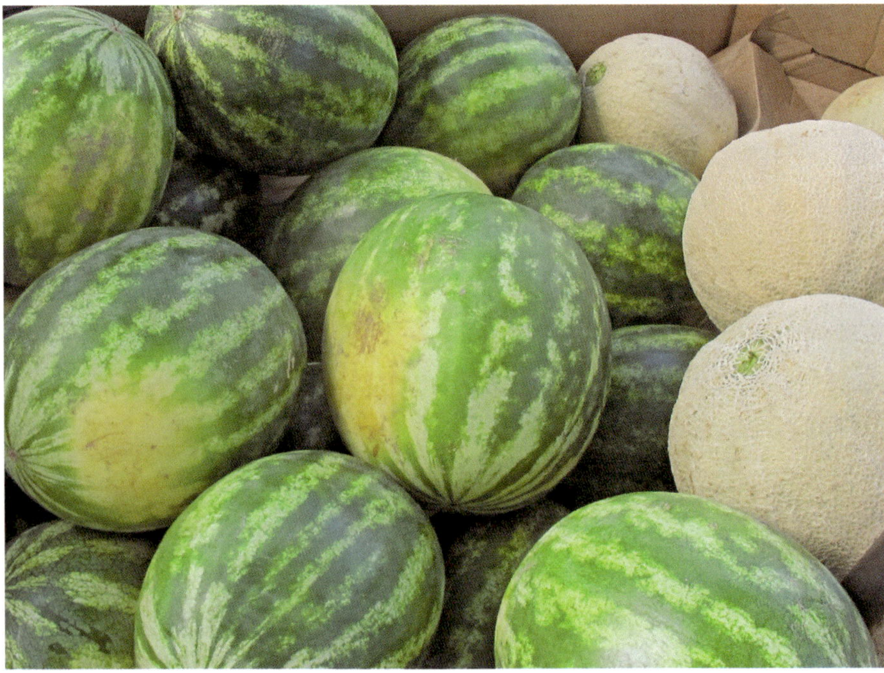

Kalmar Farm watermelon and cantaloupe, grown in Harrington, Delaware. *Jack Clemons photo.*

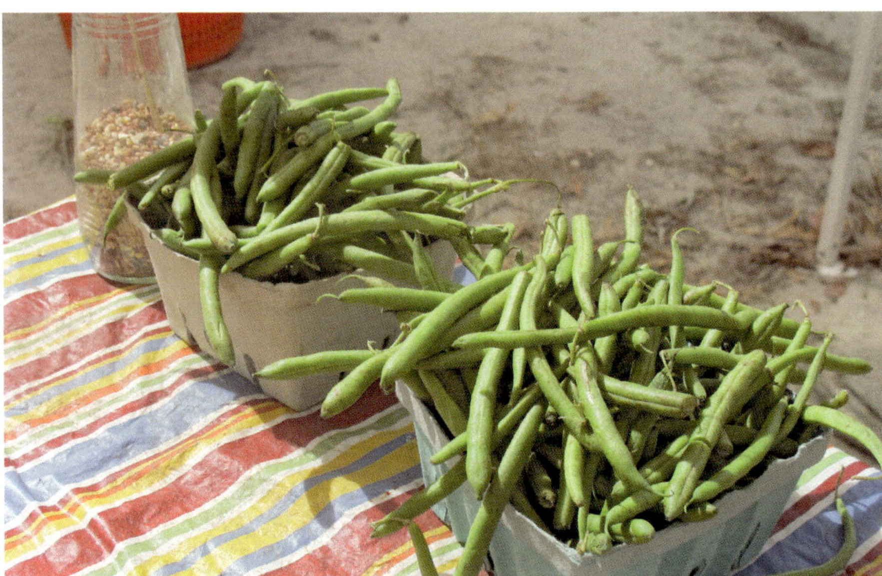

Traditional string beans, not the regional pole beans found in private gardens or baby lima beans grown in Lincoln, Delaware. *Jack Clemons photo.*

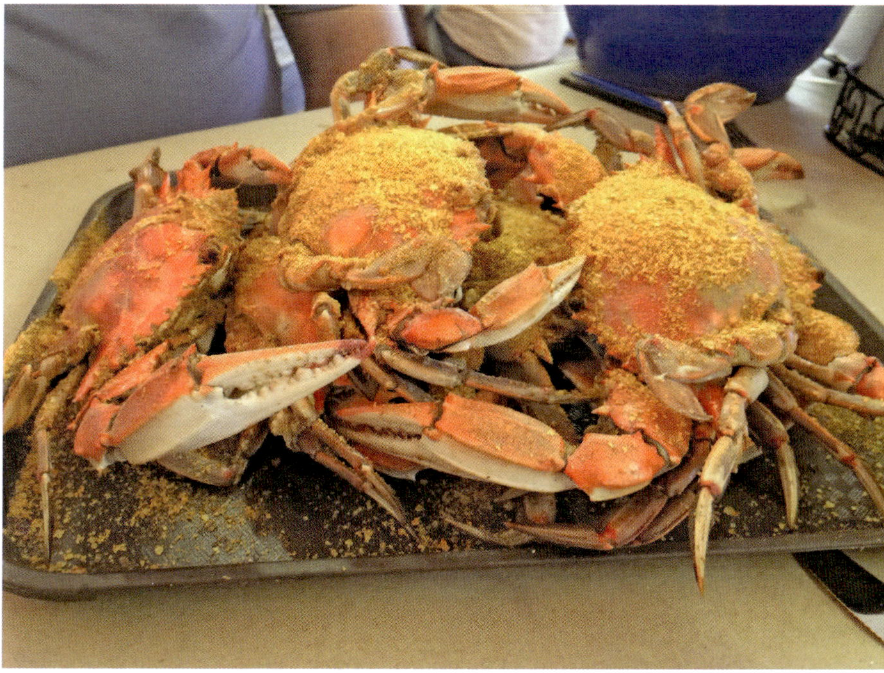

Delaware blue crabs, steamed and sprinkled with Old Bay seasoning. *Jack Clemons photo.*

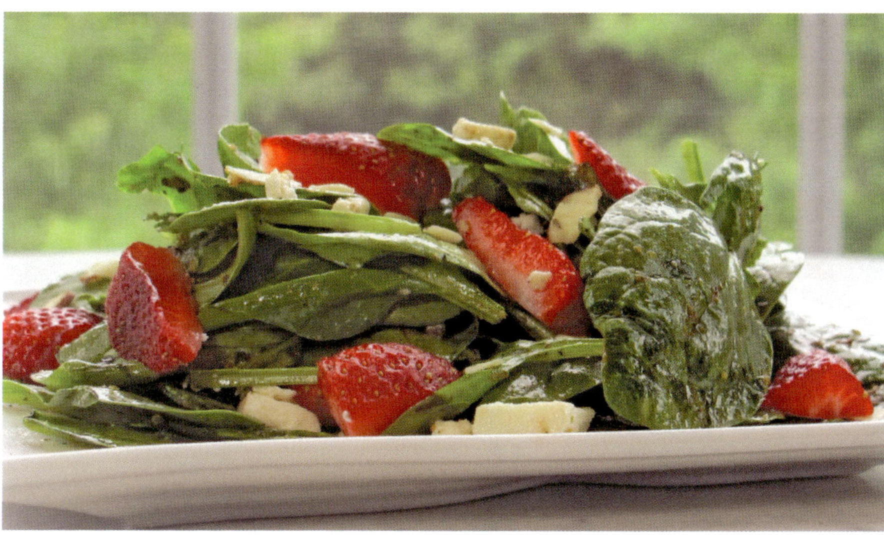

Strawberry spinach salad in a vinaigrette dressing. *Jack Clemons photo.*

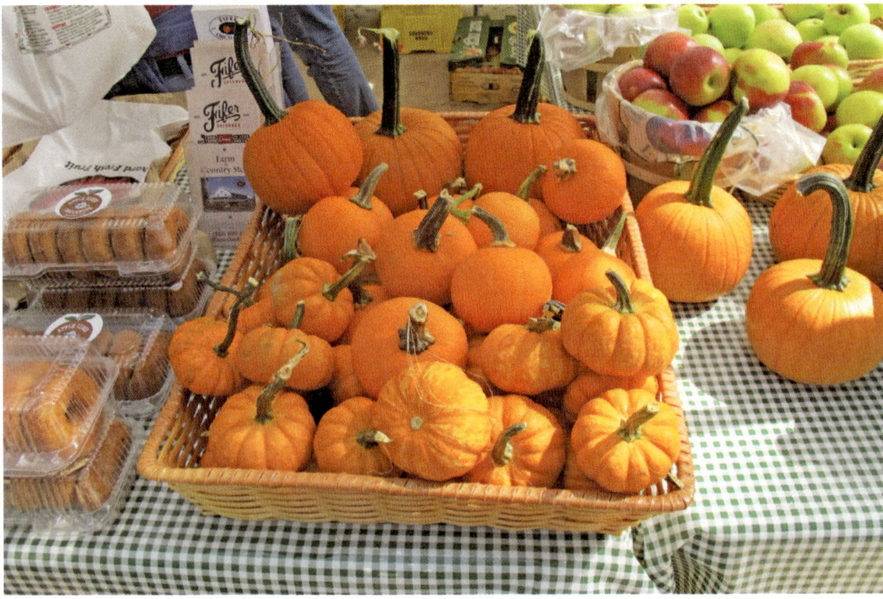

Petite pumpkins and pie pumpkins next to apple cider doughnuts offered by Fifer Orchards at its farm stand market. *Jack Clemons photo.*

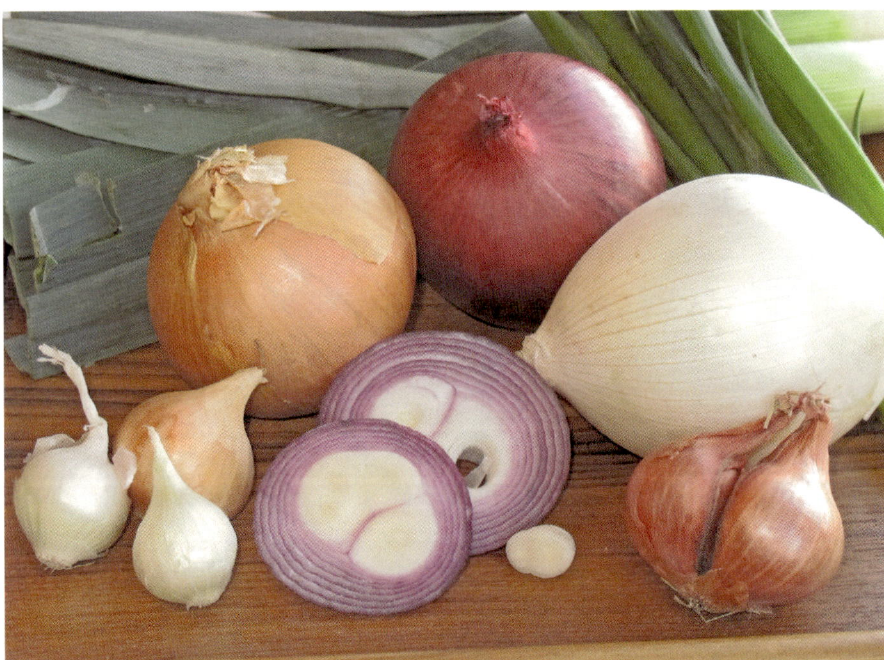

An array of members from the onion family grown in Delaware. *Jack Clemons photo.*

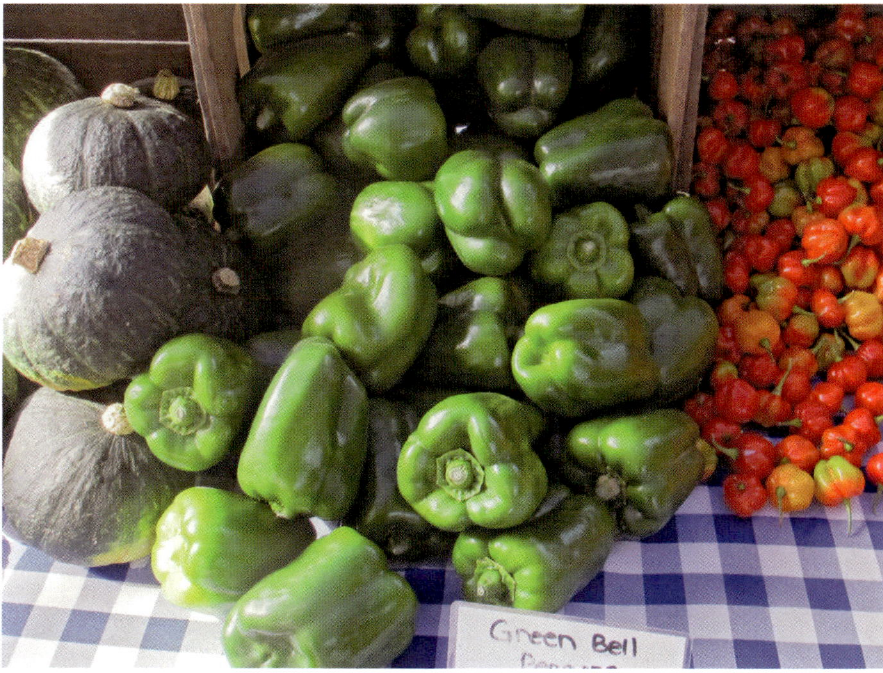

From left to right at the Milton, Delaware Farmers' Market: kabocha squash, green bell peppers and miniature red peppers. *Jack Clemons photo.*

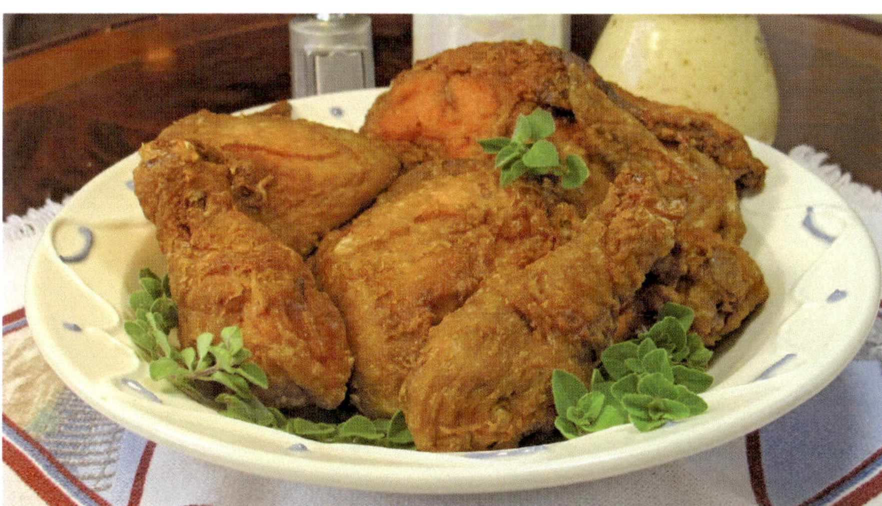

Fried chicken can always be found on the menu in Southern Delaware. *Jack Clemons photo.*

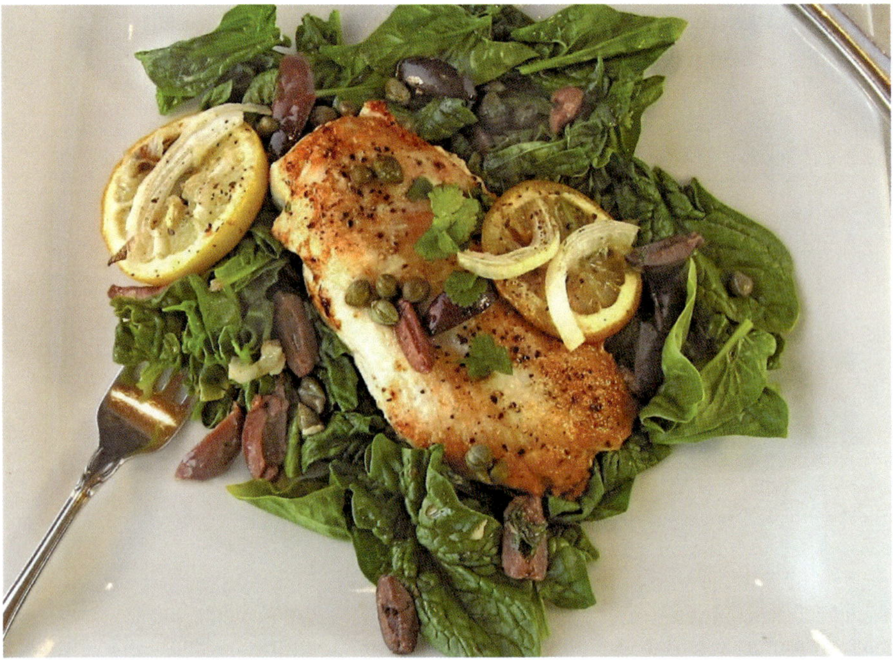

Lemon Kalamata Chicken, sautéed with roasted lemons and garnished with capers on a bed of spinach—an elegant presentation of a Delaware bird. *Jack Clemons photo.*

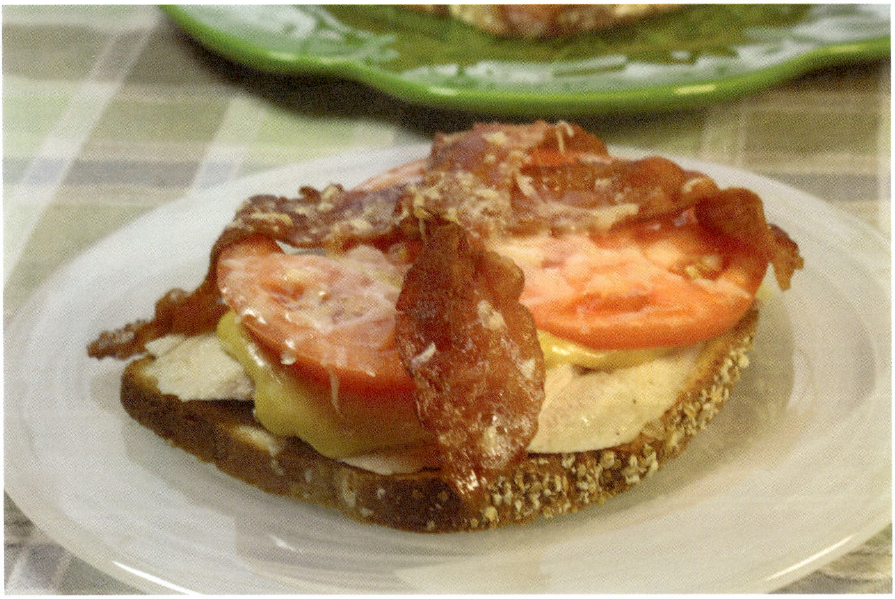

Open-faced sandwich known as the "Hot Brown": turkey layered with sliced tomato, crisp bacon and Mornay sauce. *Jack Clemons photo.*

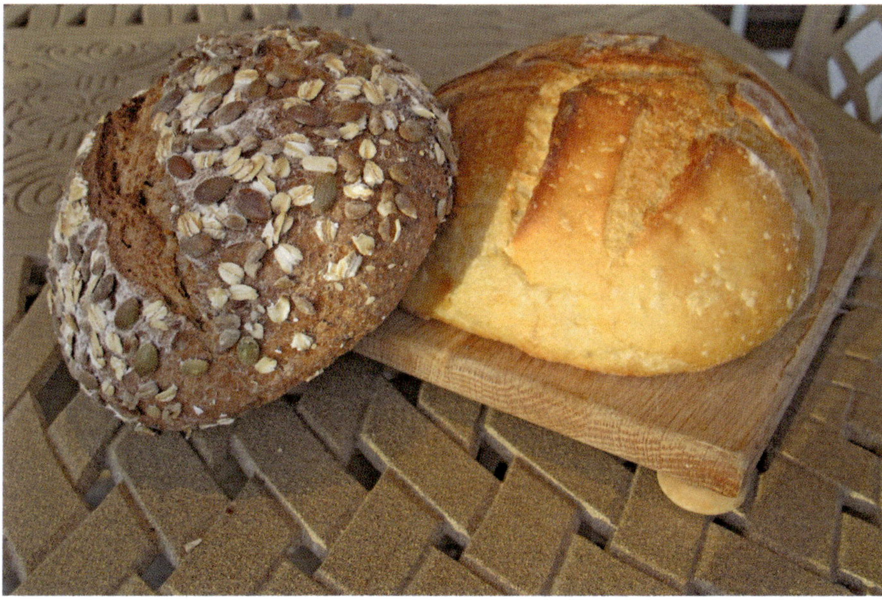

Hand-crafted loaves from Old World Breads Bakery in Lewes, Delaware. Ancient grains on the left and traditional sourdough on the right. *Jack Clemons photo.*

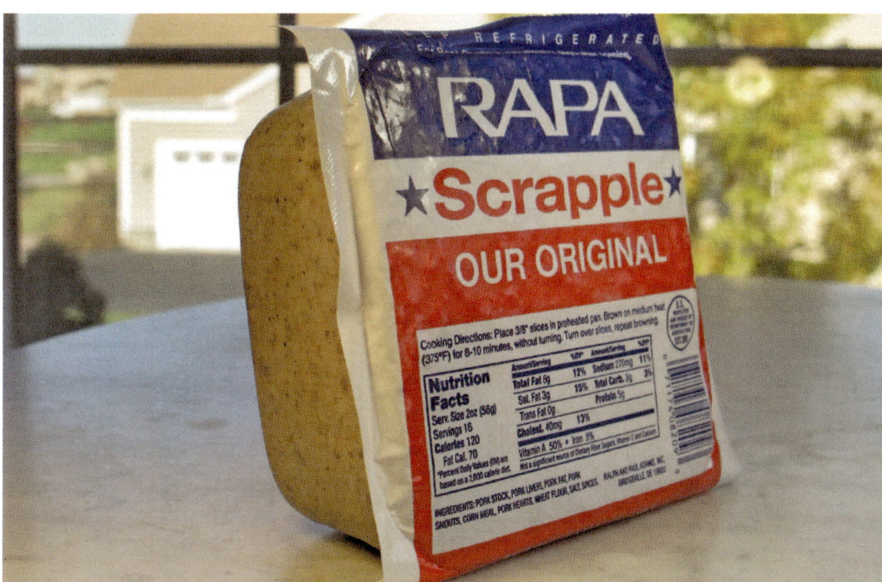

A familiar sight in the grocery store meat aisle: RAPA Scrapple, made in Bridgeville, Delaware, since the 1920s. *Jack Clemons photo.*

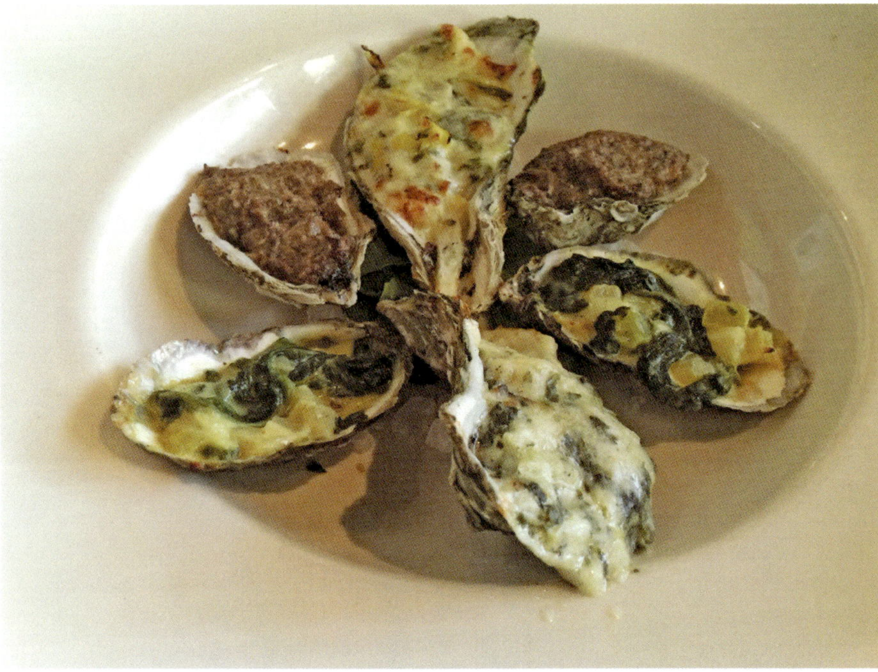

Roasted oysters in three savory preparations served at the Henlopen City Oyster House in Rehoboth Beach, Delaware. *Jack Clemons photo.*

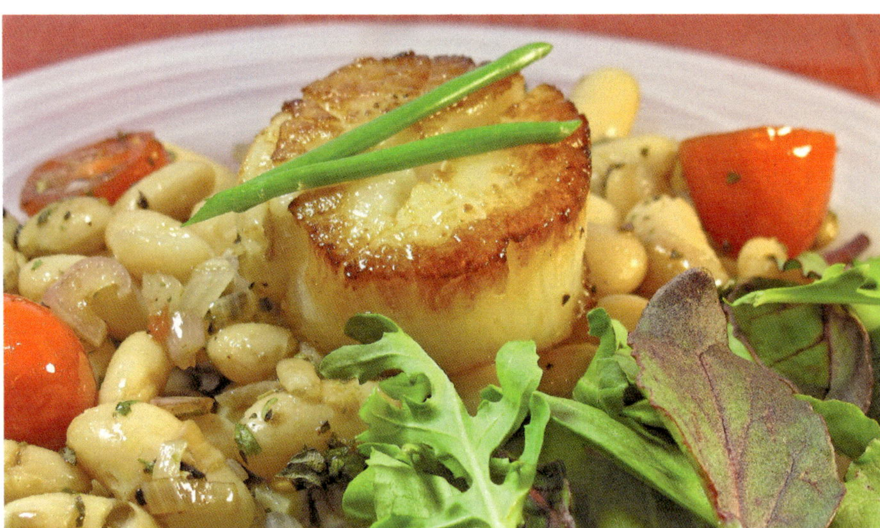

Perfectly grilled scallop garnished with a chive alongside white beans on a bed of spring mix lettuce. *Jack Clemons photo.*

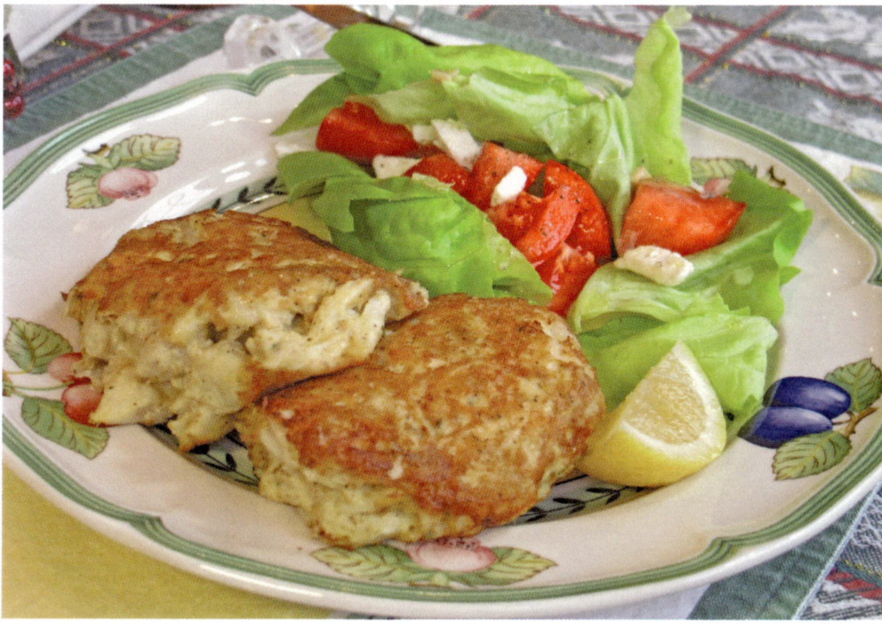

Traditional Delaware crab cake, made with jumbo lump crabmeat, seasonings and no filler. *Jack Clemons photo.*

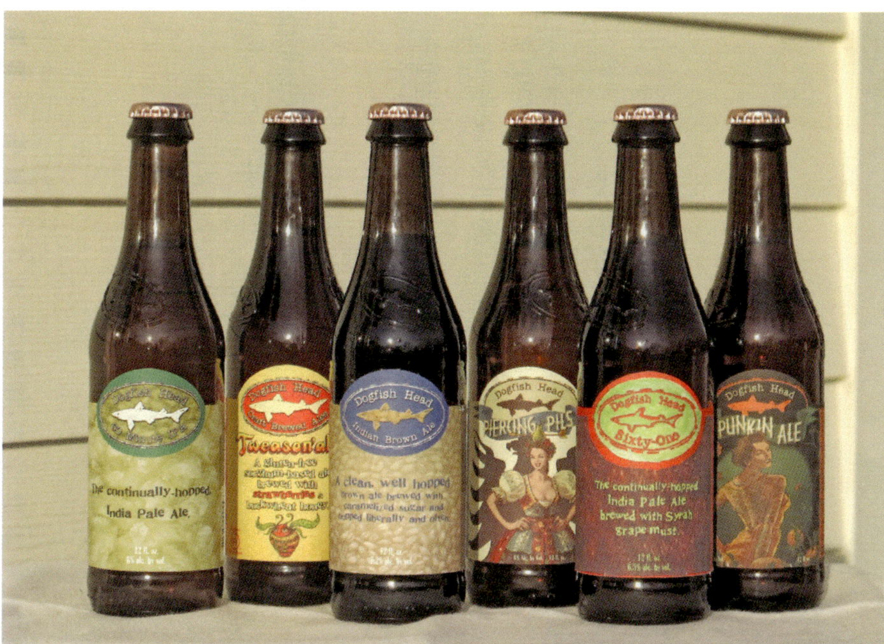

A selection of brews from Dogfish Head. *From left to right*: India pale ale, Tweason'ale, Indian brown ale, Piercing Pils, Sixty-One and Punkin Ale. *Jack Clemons photo.*

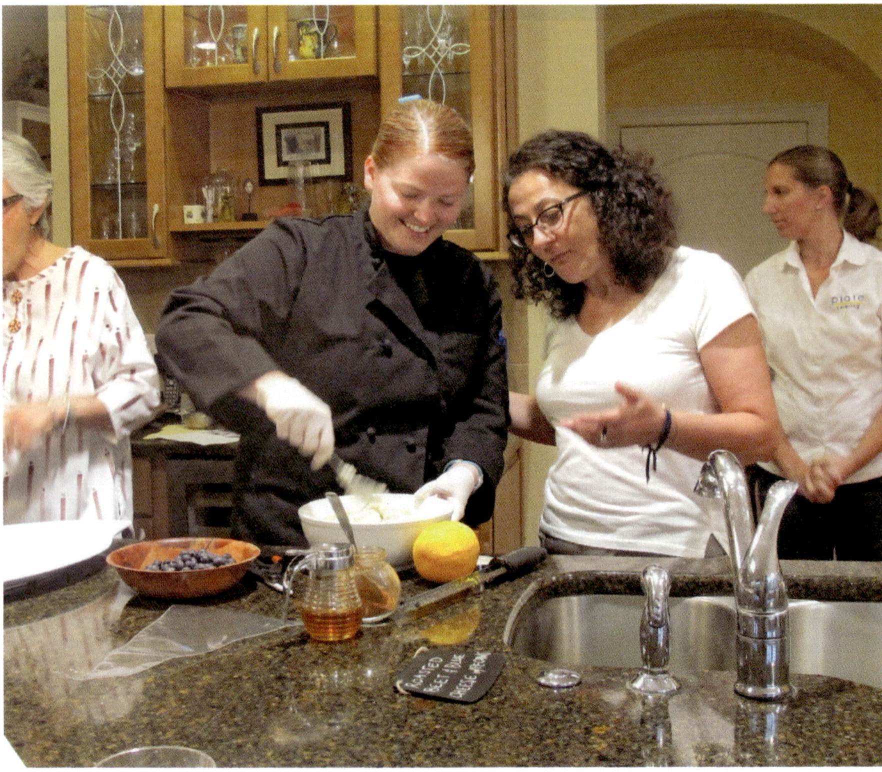

Cooking demonstration "The Art of the Plate." *From left to right*: Chef Jen, SoDel Concepts; guest Lina Cortas; and Lisa Wheeler, Plate Catering, Lewes. *Jack Clemons photo.*

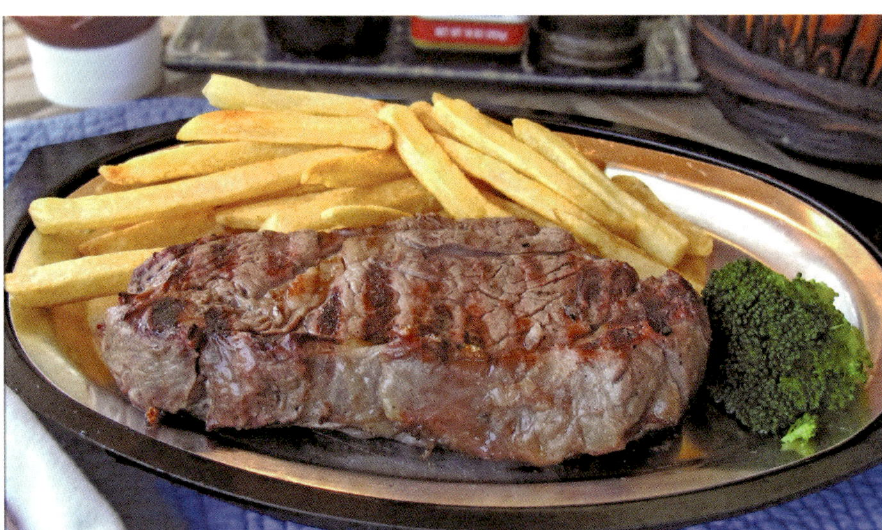

Grilled bison rib-eye steak with a side of French fries. *Jack Clemons photo.*

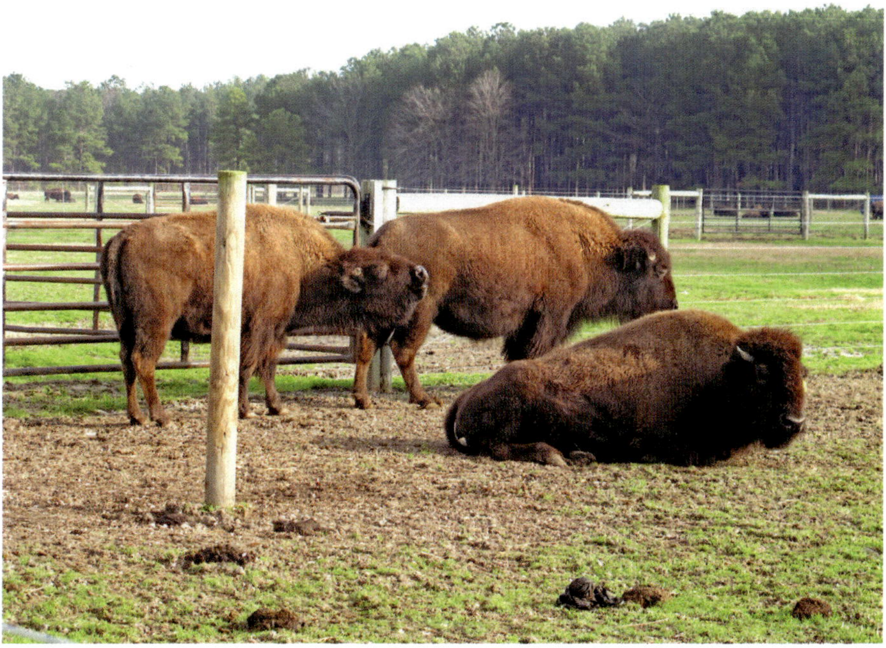

Bison from Colvine Farms Bison Farm in Greenwood, Delaware. *Jack Clemons photo.*

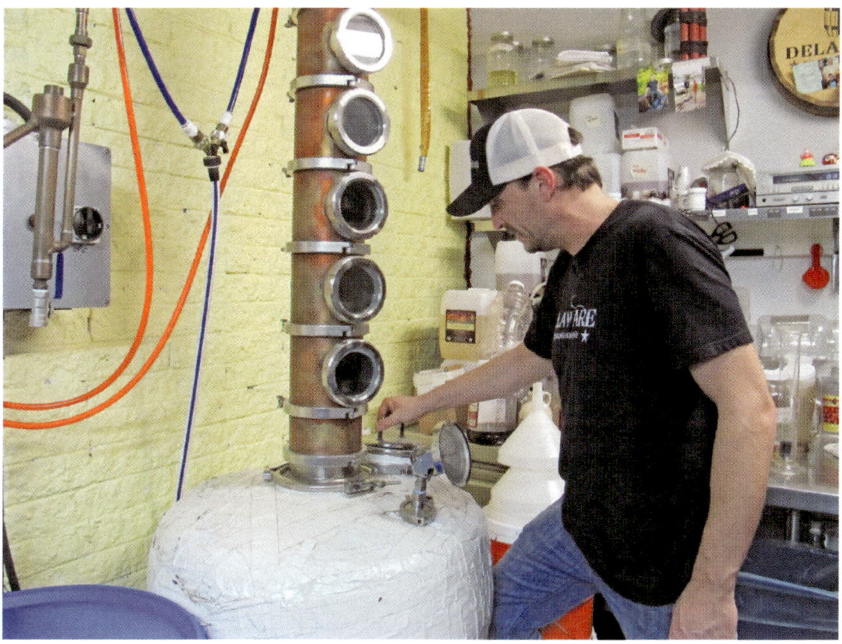

Still-master at work at the Delaware Distilling Company, Rehoboth Beach, Delaware. *Jack Clemons photo.*

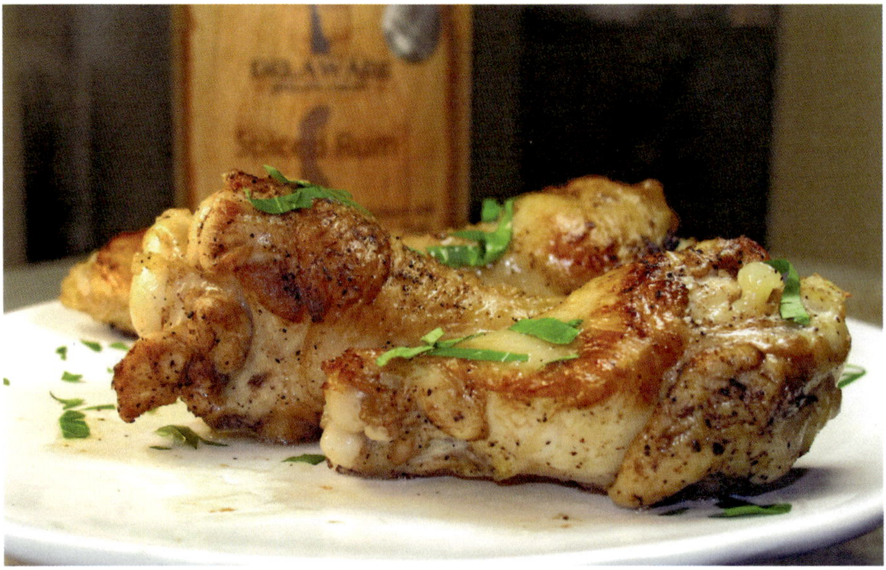

Marinated chicken wings simmered in Delaware Distilling Company's Spiced Rum. *Jack Clemons photo.*

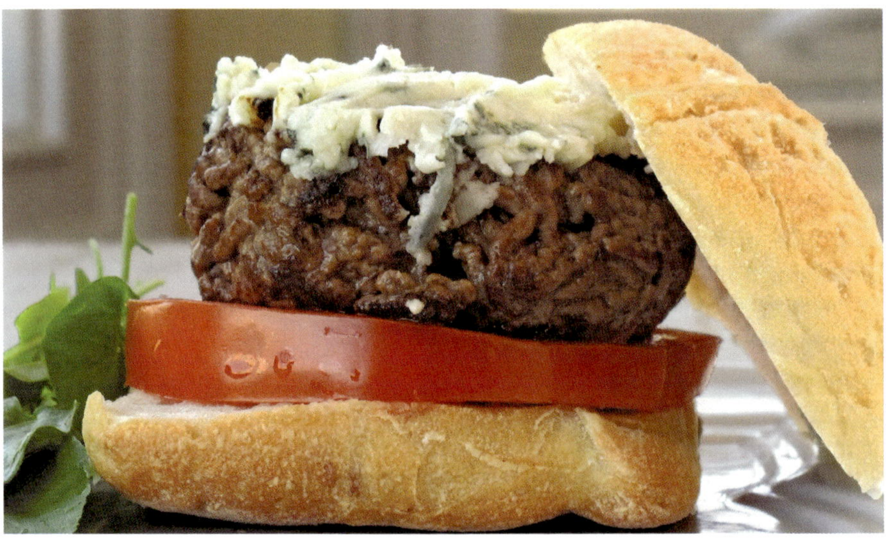

Hamburger made with Hazel Brittingham's favorite cut of grass-fed Delaware beef: round steak ground. *Jack Clemons photo.*

the starter (also called sponge) was used to make a loaf of bread, a piece of it was kept and fed with flour to produce the next batch of loaves.

While it is time consuming to bake bread—the steps can take almost two days to complete—it is not at all difficult. Yeast from the starter was fed with more flour, the dough was kneaded several times and set aside to rise at least two or three times before the loaf was baked, initially in a beehive oven built into the side of the fireplace and, in later years, in the ovens of coal-burning stoves.

Everyone must have known how to bake bread. There are no recipes for loaf bread in the first published cookbooks, whether printed in the newly settled country or imported from England. You will find instructions for pastries, cakes, pies and tarts, but none of these early manuals written for the housewife includes recipes for baking bread. It was not until the 1841 edition of Sarah Hale's book *The Good Housekeeper* that the bread-baking process was described.

In addition to her recipe, she also advised that grain, especially wheat, should be washed and dried at the grower's farm before transporting any quantity to the mill to be ground. She cautioned against potentially unscrupulous vendors of flour sold in barrels or sacks who might "swell its bulk and weight." The list of fillers included "whiting, ground stones, and bones and plaster of Paris." These warnings were followed by specific tests to determine if the flour had been adulterated and then described in exacting detail how to bake several loaves of bread in a wood-fired oven.

Through the years, commercial bakeries became established, offering families the convenience of buying bread instead of baking it. One of the most popular of these in Southern Delaware was Bond Bread, which first appeared in the 1940s. It offered door-to-door delivery of freshly baked loaves, doughnuts and shortbread cookies called Sandy Tricks for the emblems of the four playing-card suits pressed into the tops.

Over time, as commercial bakeries consolidated, delivery of fresh bread disappeared. To speed up the baking process and extend supermarket shelf life, bread makers relied on preservatives and dough conditioners not found in original home-baked bread. Today, a visit to the bakery aisle of any modern supermarket reveals a startling array of bread offerings: whole wheat, cracked wheat, potato bread, raisin bread and more. The flaccid white bread of the last half of the twentieth century is now undergoing a transformation. Many brands tout the absence of offensive ingredients such as high-fructose corn syrup and the inclusion of additional fiber and whole grains.

In a return to the traditions of earlier times, a number of artisanal bakers have emerged in the region, advertising the use of wild yeast strains to flavor their loaves of tangy sourdough.

Barley

Barley is the oldest cultivated grain in the world and was an essential crop during the colonial era, grown on farmland throughout Southern Delaware. This grain has been a nutritional resource for thousands of years in foods such as cereals, bread and soups, and it can be seen in the diets of countries around the globe. English settlers imported barley when they arrived in North America during the seventeenth century. As a key ingredient in beer brewing, malted barley will be featured in a later chapter.

While barley is easy to cultivate, it requires processing once it has been harvested. The various types of barley and barley-related ingredients are named according to how the grain has been processed.

- hulled barley or barley groats: the tough outermost hull is removed, leaving a highly nutritious, chewy grain that requires pre-soaking and long cooking times.
- pot or Scotch barley: the grains are polished to remove the hull and little else before being coarsely ground. It is well suited as a puffed grain and thickening agent in soups, hence its name.
- pearl barley: after the hull is removed, a steam-based pearling or polishing process is used to remove the outer bran layer and often some of the grain itself. Pearl barley can be one of several sizes: regular, medium, fine and baby. As the size decreases, so does the nutritional profile. Pearl barley is less chewy and cooks more quickly than hulled or pot barley.
- barley flakes or rolled barley: similar in shape to rolled oats, the barley grains are sliced and flattened, typically used as a hot cereal.
- barley grits: the grains are toasted and cracked into coarse pieces.
- barley flour: ground from pearl barley and used in baking. This flour requires the addition of high-gluten flour in yeast-based bread recipes.
- malted barley or sprouted barley: the grains are immersed in water and allowed to germinate. Once they have sprouted, they are dried and used to produce sweet syrups or they find their way to the brewery to add a signature flavor to beer.

Since the grain was the only portion of the barley plant considered food, farmers also used the stalks in animal stalls and pastures for straw bedding. Another use of the barley straw is the modern solution for algae control in ponds. Through the years, barley continues to be grown for its importance in the beer industry, as animal feed and as a healthy whole grain popular today.

One of the earliest and widest uses of barley was an herbal tea concoction called barley water. Designed to bring health and strength to invalids and athletes alike, it is made by boiling pearl barley in water with lemon peel. The liquid is strained into a cup, cooled and mixed with sugar (or honey) and lemon juice. The boiled barley is retained, mashed into a paste and served as an easy-to-digest food to aid in the invalid's recovery. As another of many food trends returning from the past, barley water has been touted as a wholesome and fortifying ingredient in the modern diet.

Recipes

Beaten Biscuits

Also known as Sunday biscuits because of the time required to make them, these are the type of biscuits made from wheat flour before leavening agents such as baking powder and baking soda were invented. The process of continuously beating and folding the dough introduces air pockets, which will cause the biscuits to rise slightly when baked. Early recipes often instructed the use of the side of an axe head to pound the dough, but any heavy item will suffice. By the end of the nineteenth century, a mechanical device similar in design to a clothes wringer was patented to repeatedly pull the dough between two rollers until the desired texture was achieved. Once baked, these will have the consistency of a tender cracker rather than the familiar fluffiness of a buttermilk biscuit.

2 cups flour
½ teaspoon salt
¼ cup solid vegetable shortening
½ cup cold milk

Preheat oven to 325 F. Line a baking sheet with parchment paper and set aside. Sift together the flour and salt into a large mixing bowl. Work in the shortening with your fingers or a pastry blender until it resembles cornmeal. Form a well in the center and pour in milk; stir to combine. Turn out mixture onto a lightly floured work surface and knead until dough holds together. Pat dough into a square about one inch thick. Pound the dough with a mallet, skillet or rolling pin. When entire surface has been flattened, fold dough in half and repeat. Continue to beat and fold until dough is well blistered (about 30 minutes). Roll out dough ½-inch thick and cut into rounds with a small biscuit cutter. Reroll scraps and repeat until all dough has been used. Arrange biscuits on baking sheet and prick the tops with the tines of a fork. Bake until golden brown (20 to 25 minutes). Serve hot. Yield: 18 biscuits.

Barley Water

A traditional cure fed to invalids as long ago as the days of the Roman Empire, barley water is once again popular, now as a health food for plant-based diet adherents as well as athletes. This modern version doesn't include serving the cooked barley to the patient once they recover but suggests saving it for use as an addition to soup.

1 cup pearl barley
5 cups water
1 cinnamon stick
1 lemon
honey, to taste

Thoroughly rinse the barley in a colander; allow to drain. Transfer barley to a large pot; add 5 cups fresh water and cinnamon stick. Peel the lemon, taking care not to cut into the bitter pith. Reserve the lemon for juicing and add the peel to the pot. Bring to a boil over high and then reduce heat and simmer until barley is completely soft, about 25 minutes. Pour the mixture through a fine sieve, retaining the liquid. Discard the cinnamon stick and lemon peel; reserve the cooked barley for use in another recipe, such as soup. Add lemon juice and honey to the barley water, adjusting to taste. Chill and serve cold. The barley water may be kept covered in the refrigerator for up to 3 days.

Chapter 6

MEAT ON THE HOOF AND IN THE STREAMS

The available meat selections for the Southern Delaware table were quite extensive from the earliest days of the Nanticoke tribes as well as the European settlers. The Nanticokes hunted rabbit, deer, muskrat and bear, while the newcomers introduced sheep, cattle, goats and pigs. Oxen, bred to be yoked to wagons and other farm equipment, were not the first choice as a dietary staple, but an ox roast is still held every November in Georgetown, Delaware, when the election results are announced on Returns Day.

Muskrat

One of the most cherished culinary traditions still thriving today in Southern Delaware is muskrat. Also called swamp rabbits or simply "rats," these rodents are most closely related to the vole and are native to the marshy waters throughout the region. Through the centuries, muskrat were desirable for both their fur and meat.

Muskrat make their homes alongside ponds, lakes, rivers and streams, where they build dome-shaped huts from straw and other waterside vegetation. These burrows, as well as dens built into steep banks, are constructed above the water line, with the only access through underwater tunnel entrances.

Each animal weighs about two pounds and measures slightly over two feet long with a snakelike tail. Not at all attractive in appearance,

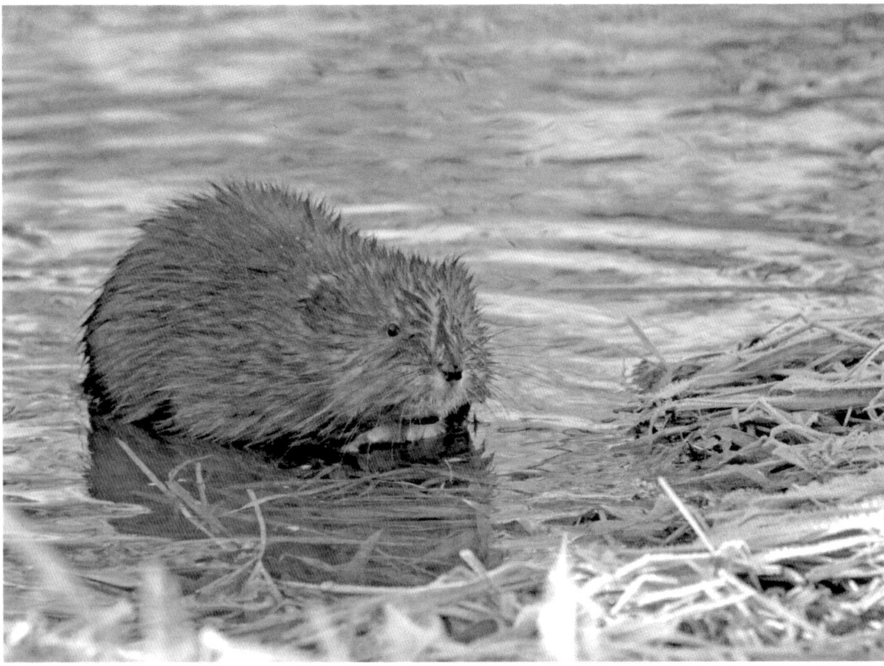

The water-loving muskrat lives along the shorelines of Delaware's rivers, streams, bays and lakes.

muskrat have four front incisor teeth, two on top and two on the bottom. These prominent orange-yellow teeth overlap, designed to self-sharpen with every bite. Muskrat also have folds of skin behind their teeth, giving them the ability to cut through underwater vegetation without getting water in their mouths.

Their front feet are quite small, as are their eyes and ears. Large, partially webbed hind feet and a long tail are powerful aids to swimming, giving muskrat the ability to quickly churn through water. Their outer fur is usually a shiny brown, and a dense underfur traps air, keeping moisture from their skin. To snare muskrat, trappers set watch near burrows for the appearance of a sleek head or trails of air bubbles.

Although muskrat can be trapped year-round, November through February is considered the best season. This timing may stem from tradition: once the crops have been harvested and pigs sent to the smokehouse, there wasn't much fresh meat readily available. During the same time of year, the sale of muskrat pelts to the fur industry could be quite profitable for the farmer turned trapper in the winter months.

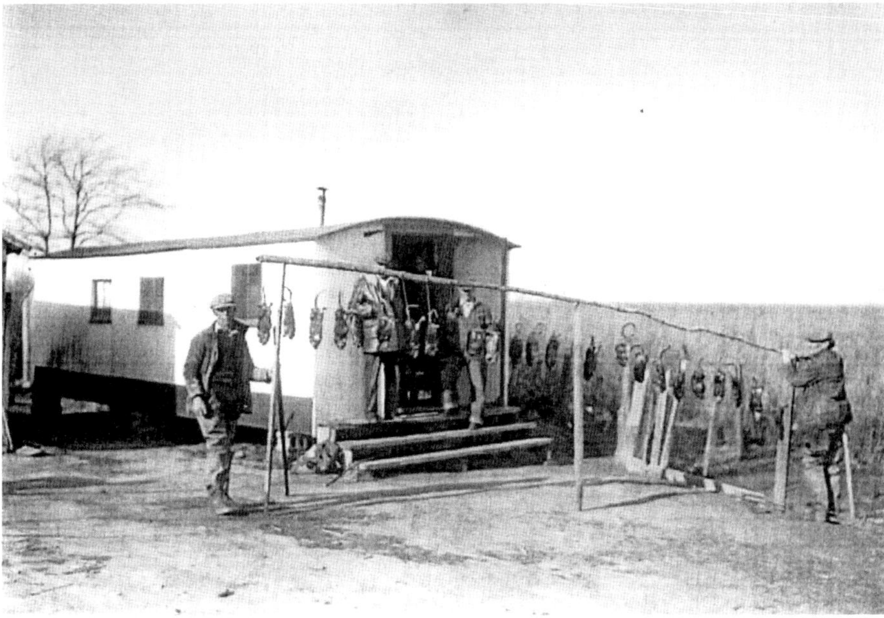

A group of muskrat trappers with their catch in 1932 near Woodland on the Nanticoke River. *Courtesy of the Delaware Public Archives.*

Muskrat fur was used to make clothing for the Nanticokes, as well as the Europeans who followed them to settle in the area early in Delaware's history. During the nineteenth and twentieth centuries, muskrat fur was found in hats, muffs, stoles and jackets. Fashion advertisements from the early 1900s praised the warmth and beauty of elegantly designed, full-length "mink trimmed muskrat" ladies' coats. Sometimes, muskrat fur was dyed and sold as nonexistent species, such as "Hudson seal" or "river mink."

At the end of World War II, large muskrat pelts were sold for almost ten dollars each. Even today, muskrat fur remains in demand. Prices are set based on the size, quality and preparation of each pelt. In 2015, scraped, stretched and dried furs commanded the highest prices, while untreated pelts brought less: "bigguns" were worth three dollars, "normal size" earned two dollars and "dinks" fetched just one dollar. They remain an important product in the manufacture of military flight-crew clothing, where the dense fur is used as a warm lining.

Beyond the value of its fur, longtime residents of Southern Delaware still eagerly await the arrival of muskrat season and the opportunity to once again savor the unique taste of rats. Rules for cooking muskrat vary; some suggest the meat of a young muskrat can be pan-fried like a tender rabbit loin, while others recommend overcooking the meat until it falls away from the many small bones found in the carcass. Longtime muskrat fans assert that those who don't appreciate muskrat have simply never had it properly prepared.

The key to culinary success requires taking care in the skinning process: musk glands under the fur often adhere to the hind flesh and must be carefully removed without being pierced. Typically, the meat is soaked overnight in multiple salted cold water baths to draw out the blood and reduce the gamey flavor of the meat. Another step is to refrigerate the meat, which solidifies any remaining fat globules on the surface, making it easier to remove before cooking.

According to a 1943 recipe booklet published by the United States Department of the Interior, young muskrat require less cooking time than older muskrat. However, none of these included very much in the way of specific instructions, timings or amounts of ingredients. Regardless of their age, the finely grained, dark-red flesh of muskrat is best suited to stews and fricassees, and most of the serving suggestions will be one pot–style dishes.

Early each year, a number of communities host large gatherings offering muskrat dinners at fire halls and Legion Posts. Through the decades, there have always been restaurants in Kent and Sussex County serving muskrat as their daily specials from December through February.

Scrapple

A discussion of the culinary history of Southern Delaware would not be complete without mention of scrapple. This is where the farmers use "everything but the oink" once their pigs are butchered. After removing all the desirable cuts for baking, smoking or curing, what remains are the organs and the head, much of which goes into scrapple.

Simply described, scrapple is a sausage-like breakfast meat composed of pork scraps, cornmeal and seasonings. The concept is straightforward. First, boil the pig's head, liver and heart. Strain the pork broth, discard the bones and grind the trimmings of cooked meat. The broth and ground meats are combined with spices and cornmeal, boiled into a thick mush and poured into loaf pans to harden. To serve, thin slices are cut from the loaf and fried in melted fat. The crisp slices are then layered in breakfast sandwiches with fried eggs and melted cheese, served between slices of white bread with a dollop of ketchup or placed on the breakfast plate under a puddle of maple syrup.

Despite the notion that scrapple offers a destination for the inedible parts of the pig, everything in scrapple is nutritious and (to aficionados) flavorful. Food historians agree that scrapple has its origins in sixteenth-century German blood puddings called *panhas* and Celtic *panna*, the latter referring to the specific vessel in which the meat and grain mixture is cooked. European settlers in Southern Delaware brought with them this thrifty

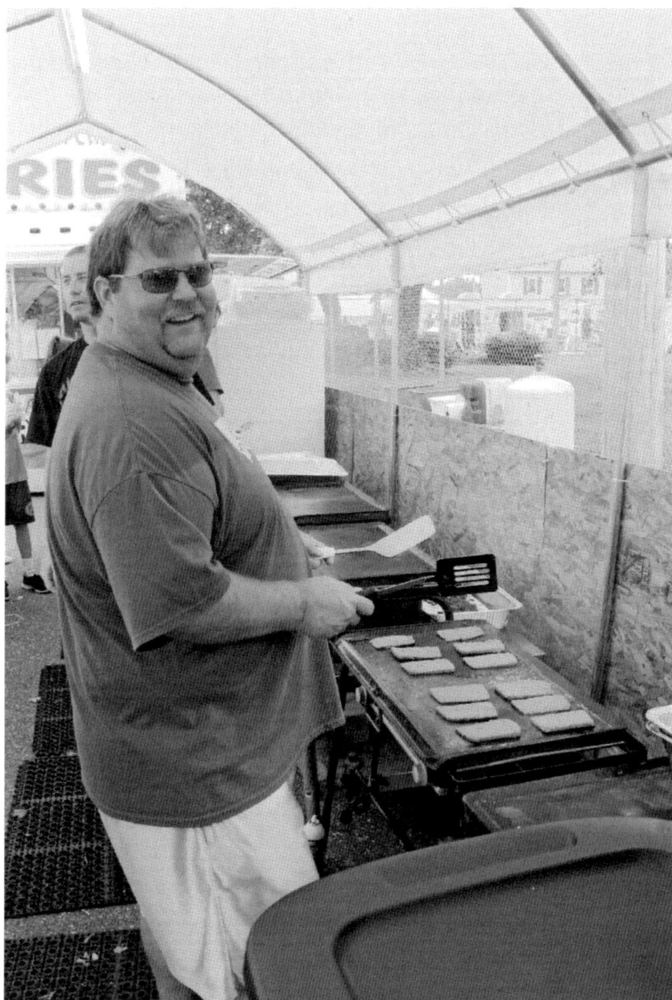

An enthusiastic scrapple fryer at the 2015 Apple Scrapple Festival in Bridgeville. *Jack Clemons photo.*

approach to making good use of all the parts of the butchered pigs, changing a few things along the way.

The primary difference between the German and American versions is the elimination of the pig's blood and the use of locally grown grains such as buckwheat and cornmeal instead of European grains. The choice of spices in this country are typically sage and black pepper. The name's evolution from *panhas* to scrapple reflects the English word *scrap* and the German *scrabbel*, both of which refer to leftover bits of food, with the possible influence of *panhaskroppel*, which translates from a German dialect to describe a slice of the delicacy.

Initially, scrapple was prepared in the kitchens of family farms and served as a hot porridge to workers during the pig slaughtering days. As commercial slaughterhouses appeared in some of the more densely populated urban areas, scrapple became a byproduct of the pork industry. One of the earliest scrapple producers was a team of two brothers, Ralph and Paul Adams, who developed a recipe for scrapple that they began manufacturing in 1926 at their RAPA Scrapple plant in Bridgeville, Delaware, still in operation today.

When asked to describe the taste of scrapple, responders vary in their enthusiasm. Local fans who grew up eating scrapple still seek out scrapple breakfast sandwiches at gas station convenience markets or their own breakfast tables. They describe the texture of perfectly fried scrapple as crisp on the outside and creamy on the inside, bursting with a rich, peppery flavor. Local detractors who grew up eating scrapple will admit that their former enjoyment of syrup-soaked squares of the iconic breakfast meat has been overtaken by dismay after learning its ingredients.

Each year, more than twenty-five thousand scrapple lovers come to Bridgeville, Delaware, during the second weekend in October for the Apple Scrapple Festival. Local groups ranging from the high school band to the Baptist Church set up booths and sell tasty treats such as scrapple sandwiches (on white bread with ketchup) and homemade apple dumplings still warm from the oven. A perfect place to savor a sample of scrapple.

Country Ham

The tradition of curing ham is the story of preservation before refrigeration. Relying on the changing temperatures through the seasons, farmers who raise pigs for hams have mastered a process that can take months to complete. Curing and smoking remove the moisture from the meat, making it safe to store at room temperature, a necessity before ice boxes and then refrigerators were invented.

Late in the fall, as temperatures begin to drop, the farmer butchered some number of his pigs, saving a few to breed for more stock and others to fatten further. Some of the sections were destined for the table as chops, rib racks, hocks and tenderloins. The backs were smoked for bacon and the snout and jowls saved for scrapple, while the hind legs became cured hams.

Most of the hams found in supermarkets today are considered city-style hams; they have been salt-cured or wet-cured in a brine, leaving them tender and juicy. This approach was used in Southern Delaware in the past, a common way to "put up" meat on small family farms. Dry-curing, which is another old-fashioned process, produces what are called country-style hams, which have a dryer texture and richer flavor.

The timing for placing the hams in cure is dependent on the weather. Since they will need almost forty days of dependable cool weather (with overnight temperatures below forty degrees), late December or early January is the latest time to safely begin the curing process.

The hams are trimmed of excess fat before the cure is applied. Salt is the primary ingredient in the mixture, usually combined with sugar or brown sugar, pepper, cloves and saltpeter (potassium nitrate). The latter is used to aid in preservation and to give the meat a deep pink color, but it is not essential to successful curing. Some people prefer hams cured without any added nitrates, claiming the color is more natural and preservatives aren't necessary if the steps are followed correctly. Each family has their own special blend of spices and seasonings that is kept a closely held secret.

One of the keys to a good cure is to force some of the mixture into a cut at the hock end of the ham, ensuring it reaches the joint in the middle of the flesh. Failure to do this properly could result in a spoiled condition called bone sour. Once the ham is completely encased in the cure, it is wrapped in paper and placed in a thin cotton stockinet. To allow all of the moisture to escape through the wrapping, waxed paper or plastic cannot be used, but brown craft paper works well.

The salted ham is hung in a well-ventilated area, protected from moisture and excess humidity for a period of time calculated as two and a half days per pound. If the meat becomes frozen during the curing, one day is added for each day the ham spends in a frozen state. By then, the calendar page is showing April and the cure is complete. Some farmers stop the process here, while others take the next steps to age their hams.

The ham is unwrapped, rinsed and cleaned with a stiff brush to remove excess cure and any mold that has formed. Smoking the ham exposes it to the smoke from aromatic hardwoods such as hickory or pecan, held at a low temperature (below ninety degrees) for several days. Next is the aging step, when all the flavors of cure and smoke permeate the ham. Wrapped and hung in a dry, well-ventilated place and subject to typical temperature variations through spring and summer, the ham will be ready in three to six months.

Before the ham can be cooked, it again needs to be cleaned of any mold. Then it is sliced and fried in a skillet with a bit of butter or steam-baked in a roasting pan filled with simmering water. Either way, the flavor of this meat will be far superior to anything offered for sale in a conventional grocery store.

Beef

The European settlers who brought cattle to their new country provided three resources. First, dairy cattle could provide milk, which in turn was used to make cream and butter. Second, larger steer, known as oxen, were valuable as draft animals for cultivating and harvesting croplands. Third, beef cattle became a source of protein, eventually overtaking pork in popularity.

In Southern Delaware, cattle were allowed to graze in the open areas around farms, providing a source of beef to the farmer's diet as early as the eighteenth century. This abundant supply of meat was remarked on by visitors to the new country, who were surprised by the difference in the daily diet of Americans compared to that of all but the wealthiest Europeans. Because this region had vast tracts of unsettled land suitable for grazing, instead of the urban topography of Europe, meat on the hoof readily became meat on the table.

Recipes for beef dishes in the newly formed United States were found in the earliest cookbooks, including those by Amelia Simmons, Sarah Hale and Fannie Farmer. The former described how to select the freshest beef, advising "dent it with your finger and it will immediately rise again; if old, it will be rough and spungy [*sic*] and the dent remain." In Hale's book, there is a drawing of a steer with dotted lines separating the various cuts of beef that are numbered and labeled. Her recipes are not very different from instructions we hear today about the best way to broil a steak or simmer a stew.

By the time of Fannie Farmer's 1906 edition, she was featuring photographs of key pieces of a butchered steer, along with complicated recipes for fancy dishes popular with the elite of the Victorian era. Some of the more curious combinations include Beefsteak à la Henriette and Beefsteak à la Victor Hugo with egg yolk–based sauces and Beefsteak à la Mirabeau garnished with anchovies and stoned (pitted) olives.

In Delaware, the *Blue Hen's Chickens' Cook Book* of 1921 includes only a handful of beef recipes: a roast, an oyster-sauced steak and three calling for ground "hamburg" as the key ingredient. By the time of the Second World War, although beef was not rationed in the region, it was nonetheless available only in limited supply. After the war, beef became one of the cheapest meats available and its popularity soared.

During the past thirty years, America's desire for beef has undergone a shift. Despite *The Jungle*, Upton Sinclair's exposé of the meatpacking industry in the early twentieth century, not all unsavory practices were eliminated, and consumers continue to express their concerns about animal cruelty. Outbreaks of illness caused by tainted ground beef and the institutional use of "pink slime" as an additive to commercially ground beef have combined with outrage over the antibiotic and hormone treatments that became standard on large-scale cattle ranches. Many consumers have returned to the practice of their ancestors: buying meat directly from local farmers who guarantee the diet and care of their grass-fed cattle.

RECIPES

Stewed Muskrat

Every muskrat fancier will have his own way of cooking muskrat, along with the list of ingredients in his special seasoning mixture. This modern dish comes from Erin Elizabeth Smith of Sundress Academy for the Arts.

½ cup salt
⅓ cup sugar
cold water
flour for dredging
1 tablespoon oil
2 tablespoon butter

1 chopped onion
2 chopped carrots
3 chopped celery stalks
1 chopped zucchini
1 teaspoon minced garlic
½ cup hearty red wine
15-ounce can diced tomatoes
2 bay leaves
1 teaspoon black peppercorns
chicken stock
salt and pepper, to taste

Brine muskrat by mixing salt and sugar with enough water to cover the carcasses; cover with plastic wrap and refrigerate overnight. When ready to cook, rinse muskrat and cut into six pieces. Dredge muskrat pieces in flour and heat oil in a deep skillet or Dutch oven. Brown muskrat in the oil, turning once. Remove the muskrat from skillet to a plate. Add butter to the same skillet and add onion, carrots, celery, zucchini and garlic. Sauté until slightly softened and beginning to brown slightly. Deglaze pan with wine, scraping up any browned bits from the bottom. Add the can of diced tomatoes, bay leaves, peppercorns and browned muskrat. Add just enough chicken stock to cover. Simmer over low heat, tightly covered, until muskrat is tender, about 2½ hours. Season to taste with salt and pepper.

Scrapple

This scrapple will taste somewhat like the commercial version sold by the RAPA Scrapple Company, rather than the mush served to the hungry team of workers butchering pigs on the farm.

2 pounds fatty cut of pork (jowls or shoulder)
1 pound pork liver
1½ quarts water
2 bay leaves
10 whole peppercorns

3 tablespoons salt
2 teaspoons dried sage
1 teaspoon ground coriander
2 teaspoons pepper
3 cups cornmeal

Combine pork, water, bay leaves and peppercorns in a large saucepan. Heat just to a boil and then reduce heat to a simmer. Braise until completely tender, about 2½ hours. Once the meat is cooked, remove from heat and allow to cool to room temperature. Strain and reserve the broth; set aside. Pull the cooked meat from the bones and grind in a food processor. Combine reserved broth, ground meat and remaining ingredients in a saucepan. Cook over medium-low heat until a thick mush forms, about 15 minutes. Line two loaf pans with parchment paper and spoon the mush into the pans, packing tightly. Refrigerate until firm before using or freezing. To serve, cut a slice about ⅜-inch thick and pan fry on both sides in butter or lard until crisp and golden brown.

Simmered Country Ham

Because of the length of time spent curing and aging, it is best not to overcook the ham or it will become mealy. Simply heat the ham and let it return to room temperature before slicing.

1 country-style cured ham
2 tablespoons white vinegar
2 cups water
1 cup brown sugar
½ cup apple cider vinegar

Remove any mold on the outside of the ham with a stiff-bristled brush. Combine white vinegar and water and scrub the exterior of the ham; rinse thoroughly with water. Place the ham in a pot large enough to hold it and cover with cool water. Place in the refrigerator or other cool place overnight. Drain the liquid and add fresh water to the pot; the ham should float in the water. Add brown sugar and apple cider vinegar. Bring water to a rolling boil and then reduce to a very low simmer. Cover and cook for 15 minutes per pound. Turn off heat, remove cover and allow the water to come to room temperature. Once the ham has cooled enough to touch, remove it from the water and pat dry. To serve, cut into slices ¼-inch thick.

Chapter 7

POULTRY AND PLUCKY BLUE HEN CHICKENS

Chickens and Blue Hens

Chickens could be found on almost every family farm and in most backyards across Southern Delaware from the time of the earliest settlers. Chickens were kept as a source of eggs, both to eat and to barter for other goods. When laying hens reached the age at which they stopped producing eggs, they became Sunday's dinner. Because of their tough texture, these were stewed for hours to tenderize their meat.

The other type of chicken that found its way to the table was the young male chicken, culled from the flock in order to keep the numbers of roosters and hens at the appropriate balance. These weighed a little over two pounds and could command a good price in city markets. Their tender flesh was considered a delicacy at hotels and restaurants.

Unlike the recent novelty of giving chickens free range to scratch up insects and peck at small plants, at this time, all chickens had their freedom. At the end of the day, to avoid potential predators, they were sent to nesting boxes in the barn or to a chicken house. The next morning, eggs were collected from the nests or hayloft or wherever the chickens laid them. This simple industry thrived until the early twentieth century and attracted commercial interests from entrepreneurs such as Arthur W. Perdue, who moved to the area to found his egg business.

Egg production and its associated financial windfall came to a calamitous end for Asa Bennett when a condition known as "range paralysis" destroyed

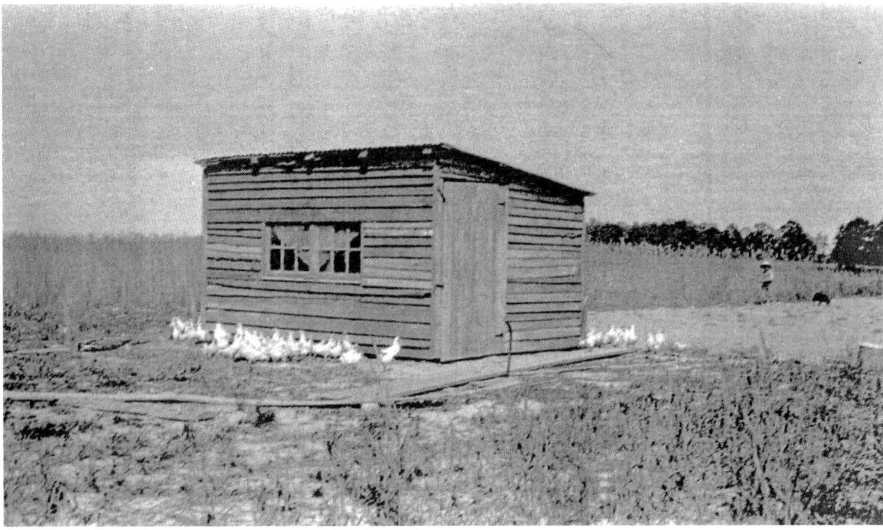

Hens cluster in front of a Delaware chicken house circa 1905; they spent their days ranging freely. *Courtesy of the Delaware Public Archives.*

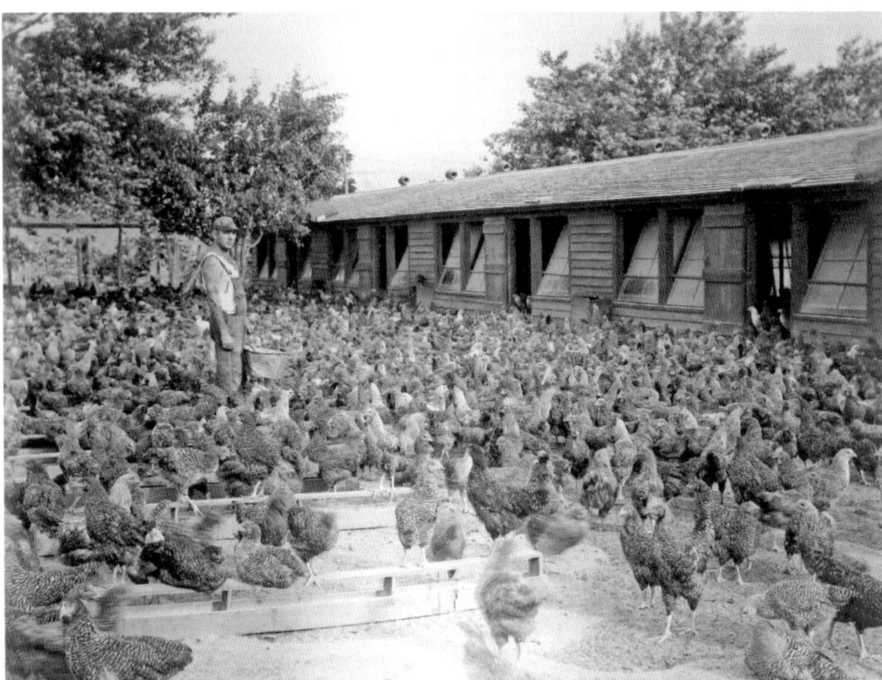

A tattooed worker feeds a large flock of chickens, circa 1925, outside a "long" chicken house. *Courtesy of the Delaware Public Archives.*

his entire flock. To prevent a recurrence, he replaced his chickens with new hatchlings and made plans to sell them before they reached twelve weeks of age, before they could become susceptible to the disease. His profitable sale of the first three flocks convinced him to change his focus from eggs to the poultry-growing business, eventually pioneering the development of the "long" chicken house to allow easier management of larger flocks.

Although William Williams's book *Delmarva's Chicken Industry* names Asa Bennett as the first to capitalize on the sale of broiler chickens, another local resident who entered the business is considered the "founder" of the industry because of the accidental way she began her career. Each year, Cecile Steele ordered fifty baby chicks from Vernon Steen's hatchery to replace what had been lost from her laying flock. In 1923, her order was not filled correctly, and five hundred chicks arrived at her farm.

She was reported to have housed them in a piano box before a suitable chicken house could be built for the growing birds. Mrs. Steele might have expanded her egg business with all these hens; instead, she entered the broiler industry. When they reached market weight (about two and a half pounds), she sold them at a very profitable margin to the restaurant trade. The following year, she doubled her order from Mr. Steen, and by 1926, she had built enough housing space to accommodate ten thousand chickens.

Once again in a food production cycle, the farmers survived because of the needs of other farmers. The feed demands of the poultry growers gave grain farmers a reliable market for their crops, especially corn. At the same time, with crop yields diminishing in overtaxed soil, corn growers discovered that chicken manure was an excellent fertilizer and helped boost their crop production. And with increased competition, many poultry farms began designing custom feed formulas to enhance their success by improving the health and quality of their birds.

In the 1930s, taking a broiler chicken from the chicken house to market required several arduous processing steps, not the least of which was catching them, a job typically done at night when the chickens were sleepy and slower-moving. Placed in coops and stacked in trucks, they were driven to New York City, usually on Wednesday, so they were ready for sale to the large number of Jewish consumers after they were "kosher-killed" under a rabbi's supervision.

Within a single generation, some of these Jewish consumers permitted a less-strict adherence to the religion's dietary laws. This meant that the chickens did not need to be transported to New York while still alive but rather could be slaughtered under rabbinical supervision and ice packed for

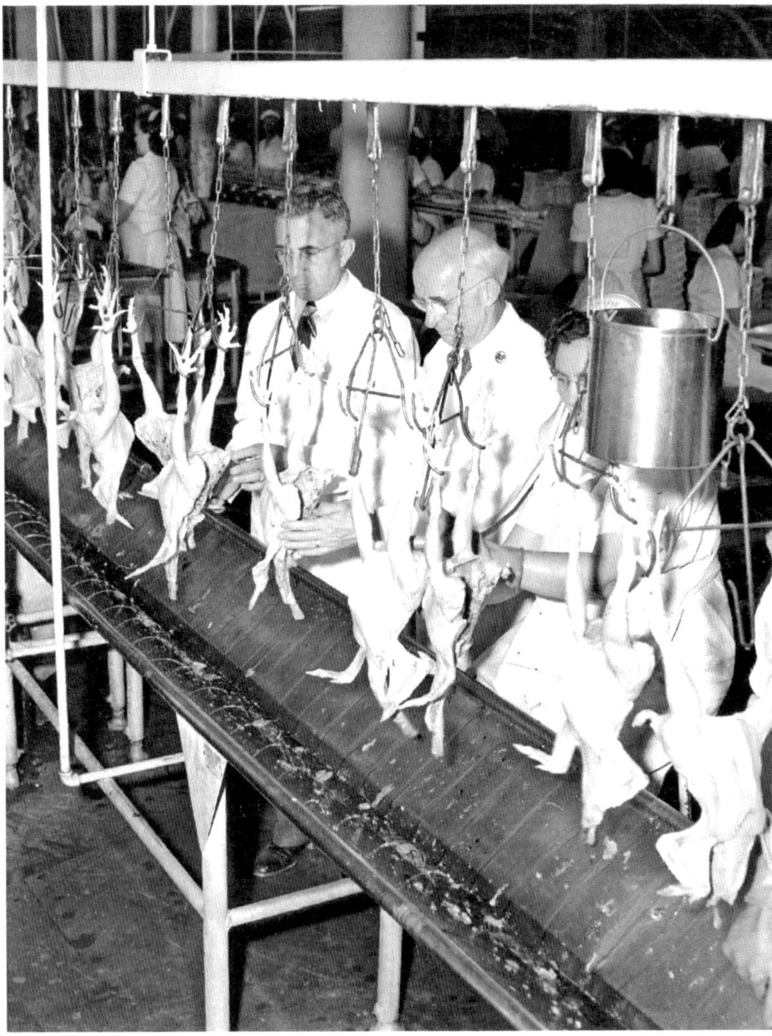

An inspection line at a Delaware poultry processing plant, circa 1940. *Courtesy of the Delaware Public Archives.*

the journey. A number of Jewish entrepreneurs opened poultry processing plants in Southern Delaware, including Eagle Poultry in Frankford.

The term "New York dressed" conveys the difference in how these were processed. Instead of removing the entrails, head and feet, these chickens were killed and their feathers removed, but their viscera were left inside the body cavity. The head and feet also remained intact, and the whole chickens were packed on ice for the trip to New York markets. Unlike the small paper sack holding the heart, neck and liver found tucked inside the roasting chickens sold today, these "New York dressed" birds required a great deal of cleaning before they could be cooked.

Although only available from hatcheries today as a cross-bred variety, the Blue Hen Chicken holds an important place in Delaware history. During the Revolutionary War, when the Delaware Regiment marched off to duty, it brought with it a supply of fighting gamecocks from the broods of Blue Hen chickens the men raised on their farms. During the lulls between battles, the men challenged one another by setting their aggressive chickens to fight. Throughout the war, the Delaware Regiment of soldiers earned its own reputation for fearlessness and unwavering bravery in battle, just like the blue-feathered gamecocks. After the war, when the soldiers returned home, regiment veterans retained the nickname Blue Hen Chickens. And the University of Delaware continued the tradition, adopting the name Blue Hens for its sports teams.

From the role of the Delaware Blue Hens in the country's fight for independence to the happy accident of Cecile Steele's overfilled order of hatchlings, the broiler chicken business is an essential industry in Delaware, still ranked among the top ten of producing states in the country. Driving through Southern Delaware today, the familiar sight of chicken houses lines the highways, and it is not uncommon to find yourself behind a truck of caged chickens driving through Millsboro. There is also an unwritten rule about serving chicken: it is fine to serve chicken to guests at a dinner party, but don't bring fried chicken to the tailgate party at a University of Delaware football game.

Across the region, chicken is served in every way imaginable, whether in family homes, upscale and fast-casual restaurants or community potluck dinners. Because of the availability of high-quality fresh chicken, grocery prices for whole birds and chicken parts tend to stay at a reasonable cost as compared to other regions. The popularity of fried chicken is seen in the numerous local chains and family-owned restaurants that have earned reputations for "the best" fried chicken. Anyone who has attended the Delmarva Chicken Festival in years past will be sad to learn Mr. Mumford's ten-foot cast-iron fry pan has been retired from frying service

A signature dish of Southern Delaware is stewed chicken and slippery dumplings, also called "chix and slicks" or "sliders." Unlike the traditional round, chewy dumpling, slippery dumplings are made from dough that is rolled out thin and flat and then cut into squares. The process of preparing the dish entails boiling the chicken, stripping off the meat and keeping it warm while the dumplings are cooked in the rich chicken broth. Sometimes served over mashed potatoes but best served in a bowl with a freshly baked biscuit on the side, chicken and dumplings are a winter favorite, with many "secret" recipes passed down from family matriarchs.

One unusual dish popular in Delaware is chicken and waffles. Don't imagine stewed or fricasseed chicken in a creamy sauce ladled over a crisp waffle. This dish consists of a steaming hot buttermilk waffle, topped with a generous pat of butter and sweet maple syrup, served with several pieces of spicy fried chicken placed alongside. No one is quite sure where the idea originated—legends range from Thomas Jefferson to Harlem nightclubs in the 1920s—but there are restaurants across the region claiming their version was the first and remains the best.

Turkey

Wild turkeys roamed freely through the woodlands in Southern Delaware. From the Nanticokes to the early settlers to current residents, turkey remains a desirable game bird, prized for its rich flavor. All of the earliest cookbooks published in America include instructions for dressing, stuffing and roasting turkey. However, they do not make much differentiation between the steps for preparing turkey and other food fowl, like chicken and goose.

Amelia Simmons offers the most opinionated comments about choosing poultry, transcribed here into modern English typesetting:

> *Having before stated that the female in almost every instance is preferable to the male and peculiarly so in the Peacock, which, tho' beautifully plumaged, is tough, hard, stringy, and untasted, and even indelicious—while the Pea Hen is exactly otherwise, and the queen of all birds.*
>
> *So also in a degree, Turkey.*
>
> *Hen Turkey, is higher and richer flavor'd, easier fattened and plumper—they are no odds in market.*
>
> *Dunghill Fowls, are from their frequent use, a tolerable proof of the former birds.*
>
> *Chickens, of either kind are good, and the yellow leg'd the best, and their taste the sweetest.*
>
> *Capons, if young are good, are known by short spurs and smooth legs.*

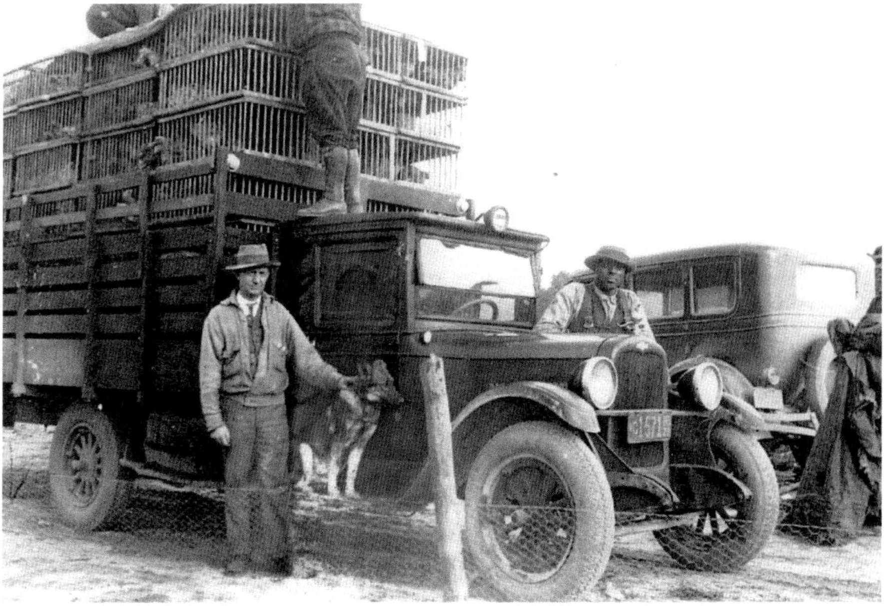

A Bennett poultry truck ready to drive to market under the protection of a large dog. *Courtesy of Bennett Orchards.*

Simmons continues with instructions for differentiating older birds from freshly killed ones by examining their "vent," which she asserts will become slack with age. It is quite obvious to the reader that the authors of these early cookbooks borrowed from one another's texts, as they uniformly describe the ideal roasting time as "until steam emits from the breast." Stuffing recipes include bread and veal forcemeat, while gravies require copious amounts of butter.

Many of the farmers who raised broiler chickens also had commercial ventures in raising turkeys. Much of the process was the same, the major difference being the size of the coops or cages needed to take them to market. During the 1950s, turkeys raised by the Vaughns on their Lewes farm, Dixie Del, were shipped from the post office, frozen and packed in a cardboard box.

Several farms in the region continue to raise turkeys, offering them for sale primarily in November and December. And like the original ancestors of today's farmed turkeys, they are free range and naturally fed from what is available to them in the pasture grounds.

One evolution in turkey hunting is a fundraising activity sponsored annually by various local civic organizations: the turkey shoot. Originally observed as a tradition among the Nanticokes, hunters first shot at penned turkeys from a considerable distance (with the winner awarded the bird he killed), which gave way to a contest to shoot a large-enough hole into a turkey to retrieve the money stuffed inside; ultimately, it evolved into the event that is practiced today. Contrary to the name of the contest, turkeys are no longer the prey but often the prize. Participants pay an entry fee for the chance to take a single shot from a great distance at a paper target marked with their initials. Whoever lands their shot closest to the center cross mark is deemed the winner. These are quite boisterous social events where the refreshment selection typically includes scrapple sandwiches.

RECIPES

Chicken Kalamata

This tasty way with chicken breasts, seen in the color photo section, includes a bed of fresh baby spinach and the bright bite of capers.

2 tablespoons olive oil
1 sliced lemon
1 sliced onion
salt and pepper, to taste
4 skinless, boneless chicken breast halves
flour
⅔ cup chicken broth
1 tablespoon drained capers
¼ cup sliced Kalamata olives
1 tablespoon chopped cilantro

Preheat the oven to 375 F. Line a baking sheet with aluminum foil and drizzle with 1 tablespoon olive oil. Arrange the lemon slices in a single layer, turning to coat both sides with oil. Scatter onion slices on lemons and sprinkle with salt and pepper. Bake for 25 minutes. When lemon edges are barely browned, remove pan from oven and set aside. Heat 1 tablespoon olive oil in a large, deep skillet. Season chicken on both sides with salt and pepper; dust with flour and shake off excess. Place chicken in pan and cook over medium heat until golden, turning once, about 4 minutes each side. Pour in the stock and scrape up any browned bits from the bottom of the pan. Stir in capers and olives and bring to a boil; cook until liquid is reduced by half. Add lemons and onions; adjust seasonings and simmer until chicken is cooked through. Serve on a bed of blanched spinach or arugula garnished with cilantro. Yield: 4 servings.

Chicken and Slippery Dumplings

One of the most requested home-cooked meals across the region, with every family's grandma's recipe handed down from generation to generation. The best cooks can make these flat dumplings without consulting instructions at all, knowing by feel exactly when they are ready for the pot.

5-pound whole chicken
⅓ cup chopped celery
½ cup chopped carrots
½ cup chopped onion
5 cups flour
1 teaspoon salt
1 to 2 cups chicken broth
salt and pepper, to taste

Place the chicken, celery, carrots and onion in a large pot and cover with water. Bring to a boil over high heat and then reduce to a simmer and cook until chicken begins to fall apart. Remove chicken to a cutting board to cool. Skim off any scum that has formed on the surface of the broth. Measure flour and salt into a large mixing bowl. Add chicken broth, ½ cup at a time, mixing to form a stiff ball of dough. Turn out dough onto a lightly floured surface. Flatten and roll until it is ⅛ of an inch thick. Bring remaining broth to a boil. Cut rolled dough into 2-inch-square pieces and add to the stock one at a time; allow broth to return to a boil before adding the next square. Debone the chicken and add shredded pieces to the pot. Continue to simmer until slicks are shiny and tender.

Fried Chicken

Every family has a secret recipe for crispy, juicy fried chicken. As seen in the color photo section, a buttermilk brine and seasoned flour crust deliver the crunch.

1 cut-up fryer chicken
2 tablespoons salt
1 teaspoon pepper
1 quart buttermilk
2 tablespoons Hungarian paprika
2 teaspoons garlic powder
1 teaspoon cayenne pepper
1½ cups flour
vegetable shortening

Place chicken pieces into a plastic container, sprinkle with 1 tablespoon of salt and the pepper and then pour in buttermilk. Cover and seal container; refrigerate for 12 to 24 hours. When ready to cook, place chicken in a colander to drain. Combine remainder of salt, paprika, garlic powder, cayenne and flour in a small bowl; spread seasoned flour on a piece of wax paper. Dredge chicken pieces in flour, coating completely; gently shake off excess. Place chicken on a rack to rest for at least 10 minutes before cooking. When ready to fry, melt enough shortening over low heat to reach ⅓ inch up the side of a large cast-iron frying pan or electric skillet. Once shortening liquefies, raise heat to 325 F; do not allow oil to exceed 325 F. Place chicken pieces in the pan, skin side down in a single layer. Cook chicken until golden brown on each side to an internal temperature of 180 F, about 14 minutes per side. Drain chicken on a rack over absorbent paper.

Hot Brown

This turkey sandwich was named for a Kentucky Hotel where an enterprising chef invented the combination (seen in the color photo section). An ideal destination for several signature foods of Southern Delaware: turkey, tomato and bacon.

1½ tablespoons butter
1½ tablespoons flour
1½ cups light cream
¼ cup grated Parmesan cheese
pinch of nutmeg
salt and pepper, to taste
4 slices toasted sourdough bread
12 slices cooked turkey
2 sliced tomatoes
8 slices bacon, par-cooked
paprika
parsley

Preheat broiler. Melt the butter in a heavy saucepan over medium low. Sprinkle in the flour and whisk to combine; cook, stirring constantly until smooth and thickened. Slowly pour in the cream, whisking constantly until mixture begins to simmer, about 3 minutes. Remove from heat and add cheese, nutmeg, salt and pepper; set aside. To assemble the sandwich, place the toasted bread slices in a baking dish in a single layer. Top each piece with 3 slices of turkey; cover with tomato slices. Pour sauce evenly, covering tomato and turkey completely. Arrange 2 slices of bacon crosswise on each toast slice. Place under the broiler until cheese bubbles and begins to brown slightly. Garnish with paprika and parsley. Yield: 4 servings.

Chapter 8
SWIMMERS AND SHELLFISH

The bounty of the ocean on the eastern coast of Southern Delaware, combined with the abundant variety in the network of bays, inlets, rivers and streams, has long been a source of delicious dining. Originally served raw on the shell, roasted on the fire or stirred into soup, fresh seafood is a local food with a long history. As canning technology developed, processing plants were built near the docks, where fishing boats delivered their catch and outgoing vessels carried the product to urban markets.

Oysters

He was a bold man that first ate an oyster.

—Jonathan Swift

Brave indeed, as the appearance of an oyster is not quite appealing. The shell itself resembles a rough-edged lump of rock, often trailing strands of sea grass. Once the resistant shell is opened, the prize inside is a gray-colored, fleshy morsel whose texture has been accurately described as slimy. At its best, the flavor of an oyster is a combination of salt and seaweed, sometimes with metallic hints. How did this become the delicacy it is considered today?

Oysters are a type of mollusk known as bivalves, for their hinged shell surrounding a soft body within. The oyster variety found in Southern

Delaware is known genetically as the Blue Point, with other names assigned based on the more specific place names associated with where they are harvested. The briny, pristine waters of the region were the ideal site for extensive proliferation of the oyster population. Undisturbed reefs offered an environment for the ongoing growth of hundreds of generations of oysters.

Nestled in the mudflats and salt marshes along the shores of the Delaware Bay are prime oyster breeding grounds. The bay is an estuary of the Atlantic Ocean, bounding the eastern coast of Delaware and the southern tip of New Jersey. Its shallow depth, swift currents and constantly shifting sandbars were challenges to mariners making their way north to Philadelphia but were the ideal brackish environment for oysters.

During his exploratory travels in the region, Captain John Smith described oyster reefs so large that they were visible above the surface of the water and problematic to navigation. Excavation of Native American mounds known as shell middens provide ample evidence of the indigenous population's regular diet of the salty bivalve. However, the oysters enjoyed by the Nanticokes in the sixteenth and seventeenth centuries were far larger

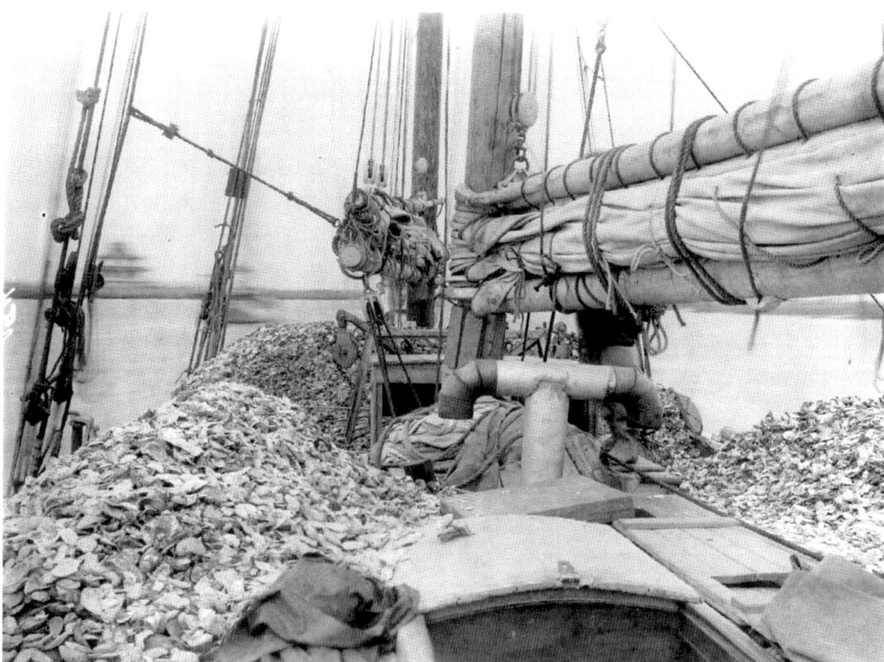

The deck of an oyster vessel stacked with a fine catch in Lewes Harbor, circa 1924. *Courtesy of the Delaware Public Archives.*

than the specimens harvested today, as many of the older oyster shells found deeper in the mound were as large as a man's shoe.

The availability of oysters and the ease of collecting an abundant supply turned them into a favorite food in Southern Delaware. Who ate that first oyster remains a mystery. Perhaps someone observed a bird dropping the oyster from a significant height to open the shell and avidly eating the soft flesh within. Perhaps European settlers observed the diet of the natives and developed a taste for oysters, whether raw or cooked.

Initially, harvesting oysters was as easy as reaching into the water for one of the irregularly shaped, hard-as-rock shells. Specialized wooden rakes with widely spaced tines were used to collect several tightly shelled oysters into a pile to bring home for a meal. They were found not only along rivers and creeks but also farther out in the Delaware Bay, reachable by boat. Unlike the expensive delicacy they have become, oysters were a common ingredient in ordinary fare.

Several recipes for oyster dishes were featured in the earliest cookbooks printed in the United States after the American Revolution, from stews and stuffing to ragouts and savory pies. Recipes from the seventeenth and eighteenth centuries typically called for a small number of oysters to make a casserole or soup designed to feed several people. Because of their large size, instructions for an oyster sauce to dress grilled fish or meat often listed only one or two oysters for the entire sauce. These were treated the way we now handle an entire filet of fish. As the size of oysters grew smaller, they became more and more popular served raw. Fresh oysters were shucked and poured straight from their shells into open mouths, along with the salty liquid that filled the shell.

By the end of the Civil War, as the human population grew and technology advanced, oysters began to be overharvested. Instead of gloved hands or wooden rakes, oysters were collected with dredges dragged behind skipjacks. The invention of canning opened ever-wider markets for oysters, which could now be transported by steam-powered ships and trains.

In addition to the oyster's role in the local diet, oyster shells became a key ingredient in construction projects, especially road building. Shells taken from the reefs were no longer available to the oyster spat as a place to attach and grow into adulthood. Further assault from disease in the mid-twentieth century brought the oyster harvest to its lowest levels ever recorded.

Today, oysters remain in limited but sustainable supply. Conservationists and environmentalists have made progress in restoring oyster reefs, and commercial oyster farming techniques have helped rebuild a portion of a

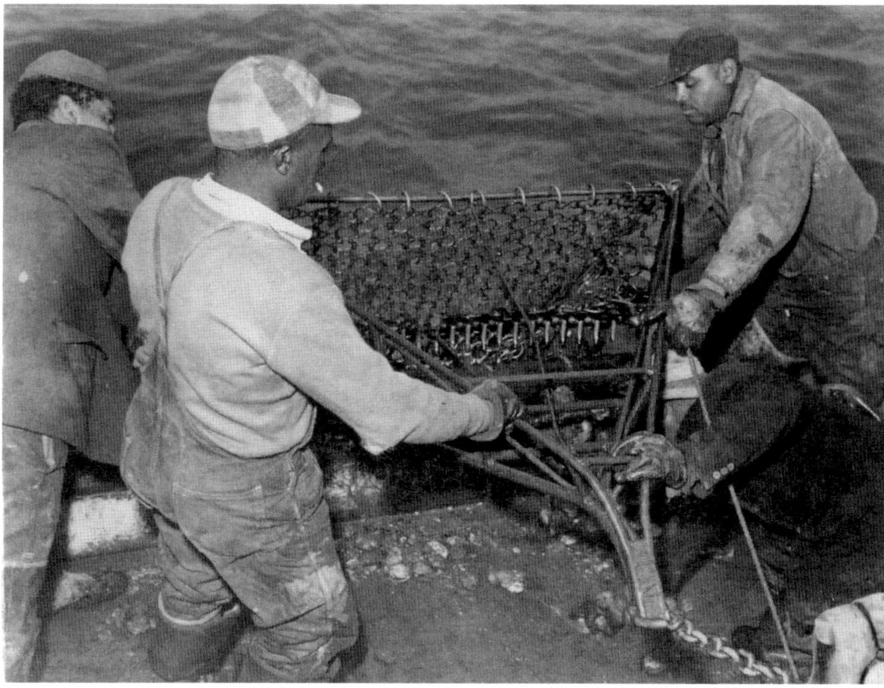

An oyster dredge pulled behind the boat improved the efficiency of the Delaware Bay skipjack's crew. *Courtesy of the Delaware Public Archives.*

once-thriving industry. The process associated with oyster farming requires seeding and then transplanting baby oysters to the correct environment, where they will spend from one to three years growing to full size for harvest.

Unlike some aquaculture techniques that include feeding stock with commercial fish meal and dosing with antibiotics, oysters simply require a flat surface to which they attach. As they form their surrounding shell, layer by layer, they filter-feed on particles in the surrounding waters. The creation of artificial oyster beds serves to improve the quality of the water in the local environment and encourage the growth of native plants.

On a recent "eco-tourism" excursion we took, the filtering expertise of the oyster was aptly demonstrated. The guide plucked an oyster from the edge of a brackish streamlet and tossed the tightly closed specimen into a fish bowl filled with murky water. As the boat continued along its journey, the guide pointed out other spots where oysters could be found. When he finished his narration, he pointed to the fish bowl. To everyone's surprise, the water was now completely clear. Even more surprising was the guest at the back of the boat who asked if he could eat it.

One of the longstanding myths about oysters is that they shouldn't be eaten unless the month has the letter *r* in its name. This comes from the seasonal spawning time of oysters, which happens during warmer, non-*r* months of the year. Oysters may be safely harvested and consumed during these times—they just won't be as plump and juicy as they will during colder months. It is simply a matter of preference.

Because of their relative scarcity, for the best appreciation of their briny nature, oysters should be eaten raw. Depending on fresh supplies, regional restaurants offering raw oysters will often serve Delaware Bay oysters alongside imports from New England, Canada and Virginia. The most reputable places will not only have a menu with the oysters' place names of origin but also a brief description of their flavor profile.

Oysters are typically served on the half-shell with a lemon wedge and ketchup-horseradish dipping sauce or the European-style vinegar-based mignonette. Lemon juice is spritzed over each oyster for the right balance of acid and alkaline. Purists will pour the oyster and its attendant liquid directly into their open mouths without any sauce but always chew the morsel slightly for the full flavor and texture experience.

Another popular way to enjoy oysters has always been to roast them—whether over a primitive wood fire, as in the past, or the backyard barbecue

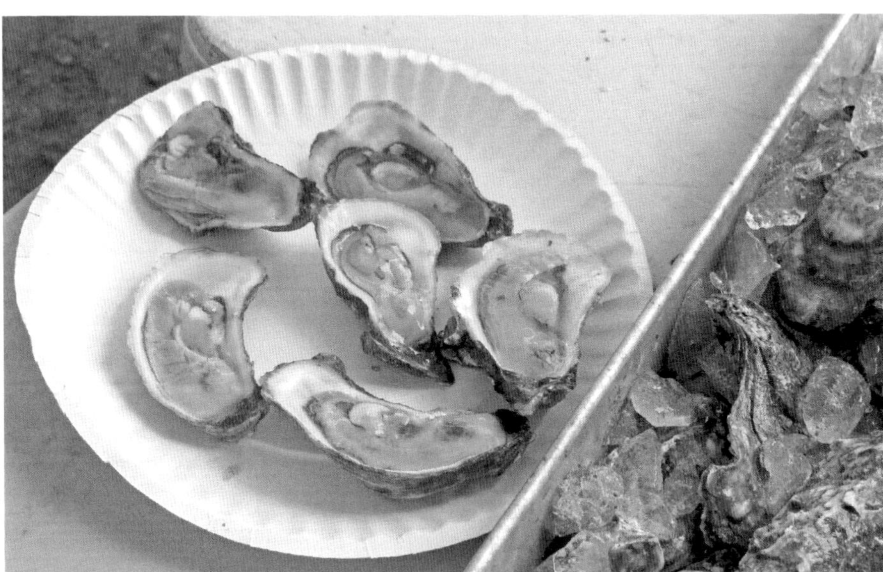

A plate of freshly shucked oysters offered for sale at the Rehoboth Beach Farmers' Market in 2015. *Jack Clemons photo.*

grill of today. The oysters are shucked to remove one shell and the meat left on the remaining shell is dressed with seasonings. After a few minutes over the heat, the edges of the oyster meat will begin to curl, a sign they're cooked and ready to enjoy.

Variations on the roasted oyster have evolved as cooking implements have changed. Instead of an open fire, oysters are now baked in an oven and piled with spices and other ingredients including shallots, spinach, anise and mushrooms. The recipe here for scalloped oysters is a family-style version of baked oysters on a bed of breadcrumbs instead of on the shell.

Finally, there is the wonderful fried oyster. These are dredged in a mixture of seasoned flour and cornmeal and then tossed into a skillet of hot fat. The result is a crunchy exterior surrounding the creamy texture of the flash-fried oyster meat that releases steaming hot juices with the first bite.

CRABS

Southern Delaware is widely known for the iconic blue crab. These are found in the Chesapeake and Delaware Bays, as well as the brackish streams and marshes throughout the region, a familiar symbol of the bounty of the local waters. This desirable catch lives up to its Latin name *Callinectes supidus*, or "savory beautiful swimmer." Hundreds of years ago, blue crab was plentiful and easy to harvest, which is how it became a key ingredient in so many traditional local dishes.

Blue crabs have a predictable life cycle and a colorful set of names, depending on their sex and point of development. Female crabs, known as sooks, are recognizable by their bell-shaped apron, likened to an outline of the U.S. Capitol Building, on their underside. Male crabs, known as jimmies, have a long, narrow, inverted T-shape on their bottom shell said to resemble the Washington Monument.

When crabs are ready to start their molting process, they are called peelers. Once they shed their hard shell and before their new shell hardens, they are known as soft shells, considered a delicacy by many and avoided by the squeamish. The best-tasting blue crabs are available in the warmer months, from May through October, and the meat picked from their shells is graded into several categories.

Jumbo lump is just that, large chunks of meat without any attached shell pieces or cartilage. Lump is quite similar, but not every piece is as uniformly large as jumbo lump. Backfin crabmeat is taken from the top side of the crab, usually fairly large pieces with minimal shell. Special crabmeat is a combination of flaky meat from the body with a little bit of lump mixed in; shell pieces are prevalent in this mixture, which should be carefully picked through before eating. Claw meat comes from the larger claws and is darker in color with a very sweet flavor.

Harvesting crabs is not difficult, and every crabber has his favorite approach. From the earliest days through modern times, catching crabs required little more than tying bait to a long string and standing ready with a sturdy net. Crabbers toss the string into the water and wait for a tug signaling that a crab has found the bait. The string is slowly pulled closer, with the crab in pursuit, until the savory swimmer is close enough to scoop up with the net.

Today, metal cages and pot-shaped traps are designed to offer easy entrance but no way of exit for curious visitors that crawl inside. These contraptions are baited with chicken necks, tied to a float and left for several hours or overnight to fill with crabs. Sites of good crabbing are kept as secret as the location of buried treasure, although when children are seen dropping crab pots from low bridges that could be a sign there are crabs in the waters below. Buoys and floats along the shores of the Nanticoke River, the Broadkill River and other brackish streams are a familiar sight to recreational boaters.

One of the most entertaining ways to eat fresh crabs is at a crab feast. Whether in a neighbor's backyard or in a cement-floored, open-air restaurant, the meal is always boisterous. Typically, wooden picnic tables are covered with brown paper or old newspapers, with diners lined up shoulder to shoulder on benches. Everyone is given a small wooden mallet and a metal pick. Freshly steamed crabs, dusted liberally with regional favorite Old Bay seasoning, are heaped on plastic cafeteria trays and delivered to the table. Not only has their blue color faded with steaming, but also the layer of spice turns them bright red.

Now the work begins. The underside of the crab is opened by prying up the apron (usually the Washington Monument because males are larger and more plentiful). Once the shell has been cracked, the top is removed and the claws are set aside for later. Next, the inedible gills and greenish mush are discarded. To collect the choicest lumps of meat, the crab is broken in half with a crack of the mallet. Picks and further whacks of the mallet may be necessary before all the meat can be culled and devoured.

As described, a crab feast may sound more like work than pleasure, but after the first bite of flavorful Delaware blue crab, most diners are eager to reach for the next steamed beauty and the next after that one until the table is littered with shells and the final tray is empty.

CLAMS

Clams, like their bivalve oyster cousins and beautiful blue crabs, were a plentiful resource and important feature of the cuisine of Southern Delaware for centuries. Shell middens near Cape Henlopen provide evidence of extensive clam harvest and consumption by Native Americans, while nineteenth-century geological records demonstrate that farmers in the area distributed clamshells across their acreages to lime the fields. Clams have been eaten raw, steamed and stewed from the time they were first discovered.

Hardshell clams known as quahogs are the variety found in the local waters and are named according to their size—littlenecks, topnecks, cherrystones and chowders (the largest, usually chopped and simmered in soups). The ridges on the exterior of the heavy, gray-colored clamshell are actually growth rings, which appear closer and closer together as the clam ages. As an estimate, a four-inch-long quahog could be almost forty years old.

Unlike oysters, which are best in cooler-weather months, and crabs, which are best in warmer-weather months, clams are available year-round. They burrow deeper into the sand, making them a little tougher to catch on a colder day, but a patient clammer can get his fill. Clams spend their time just beneath the surface of the sand and require a bit of finesse to catch. The ideal location for clams is in the sandy bars formed by the tidal movements in the regional bays. Even without a boat to take you to an offshore sandbar, there are clams in the shallow waters along the shores.

The clammer's basic tool is a long-handled rake fitted with long, sharp tines. To keep the clams alive while the search continues, a mesh bag or small perforated basket is used as a container to keep the catch floating in the water. An unscientific method is to drag the rake through the sandy bottom of the bay until the sharp tongs hit a clam shell beneath the surface. The rake dislodges the clam, which is tossed into the bag or basket. Where there is one clam, there are typically several more, so further exploration of the immediate vicinity is usually fruitful.

Alternatively, the clammer may use powers of observation to determine the location of the prey. This requires water that is shallow enough to see clearly to the bottom in order to make out small keyhole-shaped openings in the surface of the sand. It may look as though smoke is drifting up from the hole; this is sand escaping while the clam filters the water it sucks in to find food. An experienced clammer knows that clams will move with the tide, dropping when they reach a ledge or encounter a change in the depth of the bottom sand. Often they may be found in dry areas of sand at water's edge shortly after the tide has receded and their keyholes become more obvious.

Although clamming remains an enjoyable recreational activity in the waters of Southern Delaware, there were also commercial enterprises that developed mechanized techniques to quickly harvest tons of clams. In the early 1950s, one inventor designed an escalator harvester. Dragged behind a boat, this combined a large scoop and a high-pressure water spray to trench through the bottom sand. Alongside, a conveyor belt with spacers collected most of what was dislodged and carried the items up to the boat. Here, unwanted debris was tossed back and desirable clams were kept. While certainly efficient, this technique has fallen out of favor due to its detrimental environmental impact.

Around 1952, the Doxsee Company opened a clam processing plant at the end of Pilottown Road along the canal in Lewes. On a typical day, a shipment of five thousand bushels of clams arrived by boat in burlap bags each weighing close to one hundred pounds. Spread onto conveyor belts, the clams were shucked or opened and then had their bellies removed. Shucking required some physical strength to separate the shells with a sharp knife, so men typically did this work.

The job of the debellyer was to manually remove the digestive tract from the clam by grasping the whole clam tightly (in gloved hands) and squeezing until the belly popped out. The women at the plant did this work. The next step was to wash the clams and then send them to the canners. This included filling the cans, cooking the clams and sealing the cans before they went to the labeling machines. Some of the waste from the canning was put to good use: discarded clam meat was sprayed on farm fields for fertilizer, and shells were repurposed as fill for roadbuilding. The plant closed suddenly in 1986, when the company was purchased by another clam processor who did not want to operate both plants.

Whether they are to be served raw or steamed to tenderness, clams require special cleaning before they may be eaten. First, the shells should be scrubbed with a stiff brush to dislodge any barnacles or the like. Unlike oysters that can be eaten immediately, clams need a bath in salted water or water mixed with cornmeal for thirty minutes to purge any residual sand. Once the clams are clean, they may be shucked, fried, baked or tossed into chowder.

FIN FISH

The earliest explorers to travel through Southern Delaware, Captain John Smith and Henry Hudson, both described the astonishing abundance of fish in the crisscrossing rivers, bays, marshes and streams. Accounts written by William Penn and the first European settlers from Sweden and Holland echoed their subsequent discoveries of this surprising plenty. Although it is unlikely that the trout actually "jumped into" boats or filled the waterways so densely a man could "walk across to the opposite bank," the region teemed with fish of every stripe.

Perhaps the wide variety of fish swimming in the waters of Southern Delaware can be best understood through the plentiful instructions for cooking each of them. Both Amelia Simmons in 1796 and Mary Randolph in 1824 published cookbooks detailing various types of fish and how to select and prepare them. In every case, they admonished the cook to choose fish that was freshly caught, even when planning to preserve the fish with salt and store them in barrels for a future meal.

Both writers preferred fish with few bones and plentiful flesh and offered techniques from pan frying smaller fish to boiling ragouts and roasting larger specimens. A survey of the recipes provides a sense of the available inventory: salmon, trout, flounder, bass, herring, carp, sturgeon, cod, haddock, perch, eels and shad. The last of these held a position of importance in the regional cuisine, especially during the colonial era.

Shad are anadromous fish: they live primarily in salt water but travel upstream through rivers and inlets to reach their freshwater spawning grounds. Because this behavior and the timing was so predictable and the locations well known, netting shad in the early spring of each year was quite a fruitful endeavor and resulted in a supply some considered too vast. For Mary Randolph, "shad is a very indifferent fish unless it be large and fat."

From the late 1800s, a combination of overfishing and industrial pollution nearly eliminated the shad population, although there remains an appreciation

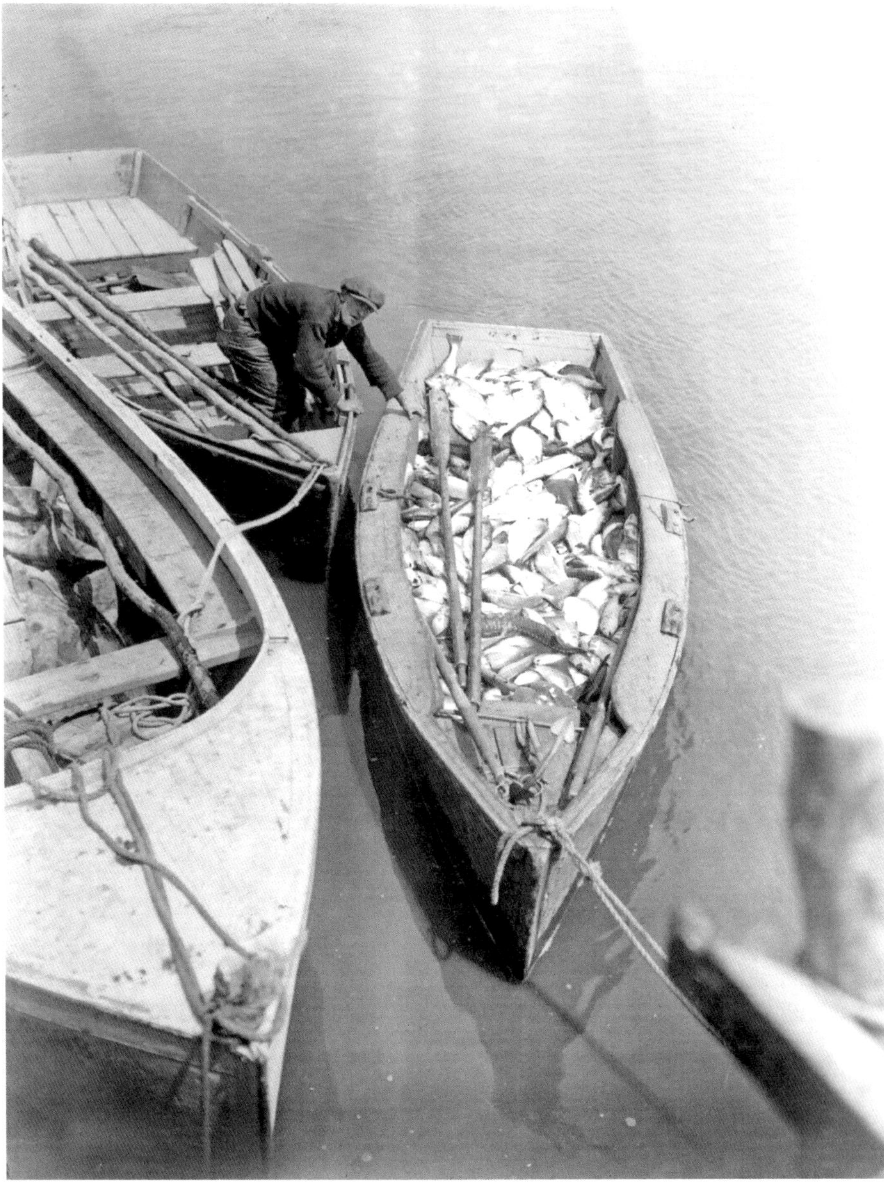

Shad catch fills a dory docked near Lewes, circa 1926. *Courtesy of the Delaware Public Archives.*

for the delicacy known as shad roe. In female shad, two crescent-shaped, red sacs hold the thousands of eggs as she swims inland to deliver at spawning time. For aficionados, it is a rite of spring to welcome the new season with a meal of gently pan-fried shad roe served with a squeeze of lemon.

Seafood continues to be one of the primary ingredients in the diet of Southern Delaware. Although not as plentiful as in the time of Captain Smith's explorations, the local waters remain a source of the same varieties of trout, flounder, bass, rockfish and perch. Cooking techniques and complex sauces have evolved to reflect increased sophistication of restaurant chefs, but most home cooks rely on the traditional methods of frying, roasting and grilling.

MENHADEN

One fish that drove an entire industry in the Southern Delaware region was the menhaden, native to the Atlantic coastline and its estuaries. These small, silvery fish play an important role in the marine food chain. Not only do they help purify the water as filter feeders, but they are also an essential food source for rockfish, flounder and bluefish. Used as fertilizer in Nanticoke corn hill plantings and processed into lamp oil to replace whale oil by colonial settlers, these fish were a dependable resource.

The size of the menhaden fleet delivering their catch to the processing plant on Lewes Beach was enormous during the 1930s. Local residents and tourists alike complained of the smells emanating from the factory, which

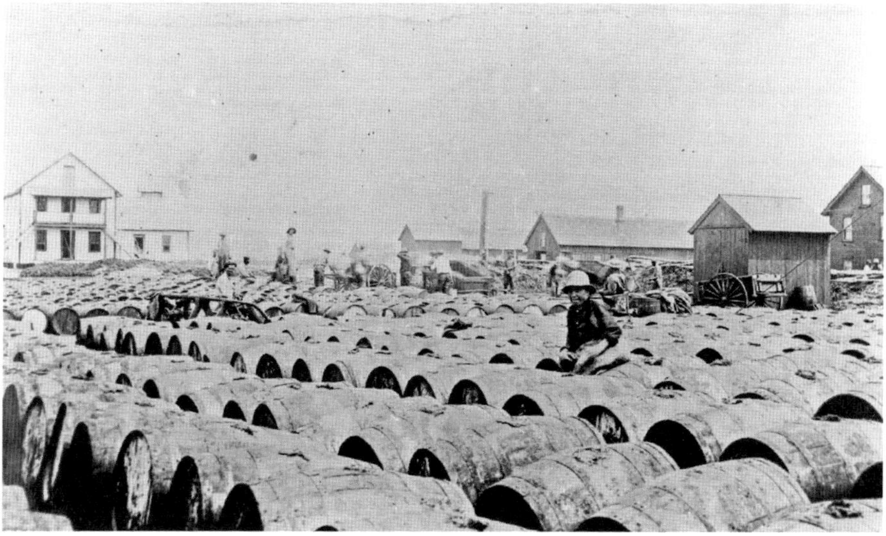

Barrels of processed menhaden lined up near the plant on Lewes Beach in 1930. *Courtesy of the Delaware Public Archives.*

supplied fish oil and fishmeal to manufacturers of paints, cosmetics, dietary supplements and animal feed across the country.

Toward the end of the twentieth century, menhaden fishing and processing had severely depleted their population, adversely affecting the quality of the water and the health of larger fish that fed on them. Because of its high-protein content (about 60 percent), menhaden meal remains in great demand for livestock and poultry feeds, particularly the broiler chicken industry, its largest consumer. So, while menhaden were not consumed directly, they played a key role in the food chain, though overfishing largely eliminated them in Delaware waters. Most menhaden processors today are located in the Gulf Coast.

Recipes

Scalloped Oysters

Courtesy of Ivy Hail Bennett's recipe collection from the early 1900s, this reflects a shift from simple roasted oysters in their shells to an elegant layered casserole. A combination of buttery crumbs and plump oysters is moistened with a mixture of milk and oyster liquid and then baked to deliver a delicate crunch over a creamy, rich center.

1½ quarts shucked oysters
1⅔ cups total liquid with milk
1½ cups breadcrumbs
2 cups cracker crumbs
1 cup melted butter
1 teaspoon salt
¼ teaspoon pepper

Preheat oven to 375 F. Drain oysters and strain liquid into a measuring cup. Add enough milk to reach 1⅔ cups; set aside. Examine oysters and remove any bits of shells; set aside. In a bowl, combine breadcrumbs, cracker crumbs and melted butter. Spread a thin layer of crumb mixture in a shallow baking pan. Cover with half the oysters, pour in half the liquid and sprinkle with half the seasonings.

Spread another layer of crumbs, cover with remaining oysters, liquid and seasoning. Cover with remaining crumbs. Bake uncovered for 30 minutes.

Crab Cakes

There are as many recipes for crab cakes as there are cooks in their kitchens. Every family has a favorite secret ingredient, from pickle relish to chopped pimento. This is an excellent example of the "no filler" crab cake that allows the flavor of the Delaware blue crab to take center stage. As you can see from the photo in the color section, treat them gently so they don't fall apart.

2 pounds lump crabmeat
2 tablespoons cracker meal
2 eggs separated
2 tablespoons snipped chives
1 tablespoon dry mustard
1½ teaspoons Old Bay
1 teaspoon Worcestershire sauce
½ teaspoon Tabasco sauce
2 tablespoons lemon juice
½ cup mayonnaise

Place crabmeat in a colander and pick out any bits of shell or cartilage. Sprinkle with cracker meal and toss gently to distribute. Separate eggs, placing egg yolks in a large bowl and whites in a small mixing bowl. Beat egg whites until soft peaks form; set aside. Add remaining ingredients to the egg yolks and whisk together until smooth. Fold the crabmeat and beaten egg whites into the mixture. Form into patties one inch thick and three inches wide. Place on a platter, cover with plastic wrap and refrigerate for at least 30 minutes. Fry in a skillet in melted butter, until brown and crisp, turning once.

Pan Seared Scallops

One of the easiest types of seafood to cook, scallops are best when allowed to stand on their own, without thick sauces that can hide their lovely texture and flavor. The photo in the color section shows these garnished with chives.

1 pound U-10 scallops
salt
white pepper
1 tablespoon butter
1 tablespoon olive oil

Make sure the tough abductor muscle has been removed from the side of each scallop. Rinse and then pat completely dry with paper towels. Season scallops on both sides with salt and white pepper; set aside. Heat a 12-inch skillet over medium-high for about 2 minutes. Add the butter and olive oil. Just as the butter begins to bubble, place the scallops in the pan in a single layer without crowding. Allow the scallops to cook undisturbed until nicely browned, about 3 minutes. Turn scallops and cook until done, about another 2 to 3 minutes. Remove to plates and garnish with a chive sprig. Yield: 2 to 4 servings. Note: The designation "U-10" indicates that one pound of scallops this size contains under 10 pieces. Select those labeled "chemical free" or "dry packed" to avoid those treated with phosphate.

Deviled Clams

This recipe, reprinted from the Blue Hen's Chickens' Cook Book, *is designed for someone who has already learned how to make this dish, as no quantities or times are specified.*

Chop the clams fine, season with pepper and salt, and if liked a bit of onion. Fill the shells, sprinkle thick with bread crumbs and put bits of butter all over. Brown in the oven.

Chapter 9
POTENT POTABLES

From milk to apple cider and from beer to spirits, the combination of available ingredients and ingenuity has helped slake our thirst for generations in Southern Delaware.

Family Dairies

Originally, the term "family dairy" referred to the one or two cows a farmer owned to provide milk, cream, butter and cheese for his family. The first cows to arrive in Southern Delaware came with European settlers, who brought them when they immigrated to the region (along with beef cattle, pigs and chickens). The chores associated with milking, churning and cheesemaking usually fell to the farmer's wife or children while the men tended to other duties.

From the days of the earliest settlements through the mid-nineteenth century, dairy farming was not an industry. Everyone milked their own cows and churned their own butter. Commercial dairies began to appear in the late nineteenth century, with demand from growing urban areas offering a large market for fresh milk products. These were sold to local residents from small community stores, bottled for home delivery or trucked into nearby cities for wider distribution.

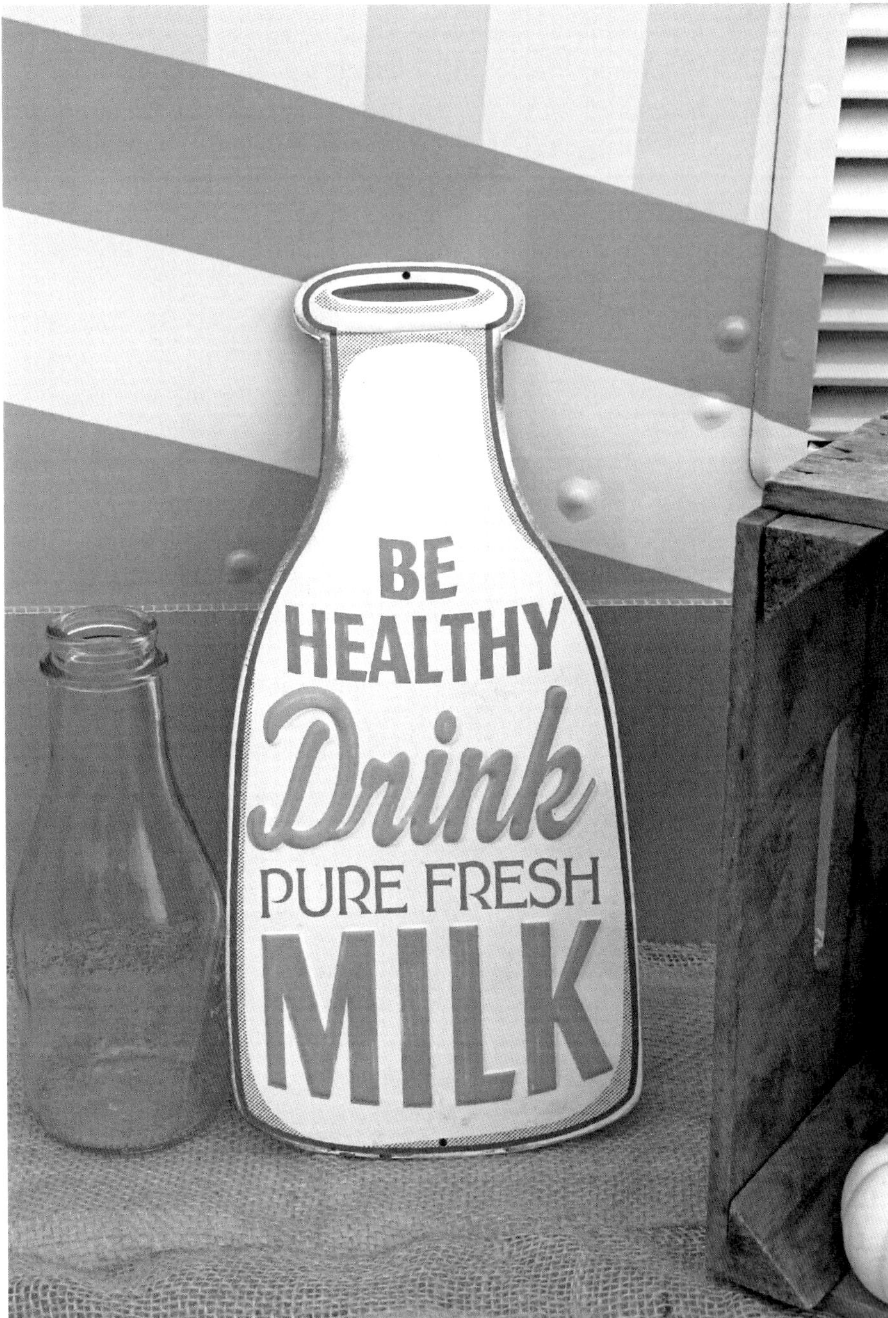

An old-fashioned milk sign on Vanderwende Farm Creamy ice cream truck parked at the Bridgeville Apple Scrapple Festival. *Jack Clemons photo.*

To operate effectively as a commercial dairy, several structures were needed on the farm: a thick-walled milk house to keep the milk cool and barns with stalls for the herds of as many as twenty-five cows. Of course, a nearby water source, meadows for grazing and a barnyard watering trough were also essential ingredients for success.

A typical day on a dairy farm began with milking the cows while they munched on breakfast: a mixture of grains, including hay, corn and oats. Buckets of fresh, warm milk were brought to the milk house and strained into metal cans or pans; these were placed in a trough of cold water to help cool the milk. After the family's share of drinking and cooking milk was reserved, most of the rest was sold in its liquid form, and some was churned into butter.

The cows were sent to the meadow to graze for the day, while the cooled milk pails were loaded into the wagon for transport to a nearby milk station for bottling and delivery to shops and homes in larger towns. In smaller towns, the farmer bottled the milk himself for sale to his neighbors, either directly from his farm, from a wagon driven through town or with delivery to doorsteps across the community.

Meanwhile, back in the milk house, cream was collected from the tops of the milk pans for some to be bottled as cream and the remainder set aside

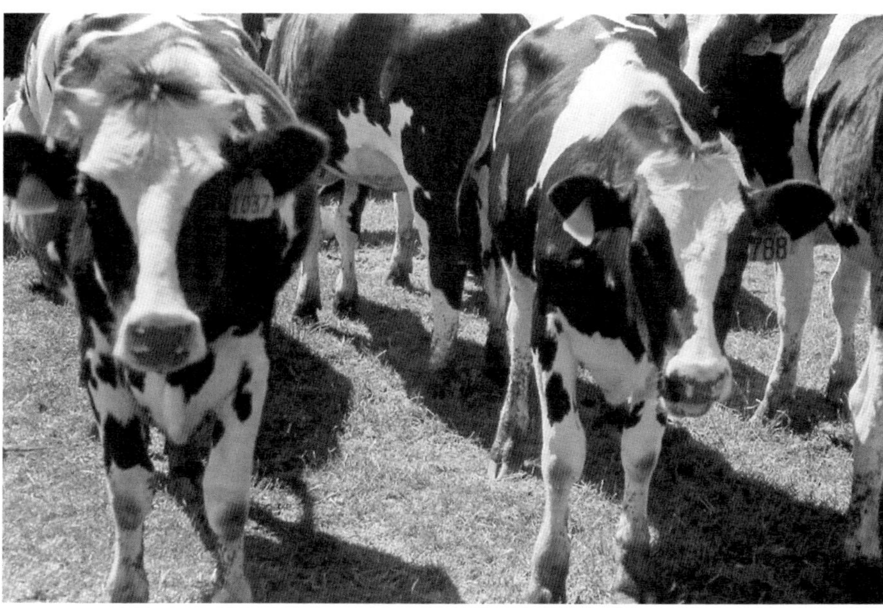

A herd of curious Delaware cows. *Courtesy of the Delaware Public Archives.*

to make butter. The cream for butter was stored in a tin can or other metal container in a bath of cold water until churning day. On churning days, the cream was transferred into a wooden churn, fashioned either as an upright cylinder with a plunger or as a horizontal barrel with a crank that turned a paddle inside.

Both of these methods were far more sophisticated than some of the original techniques for churning butter, one of which was to place the cream

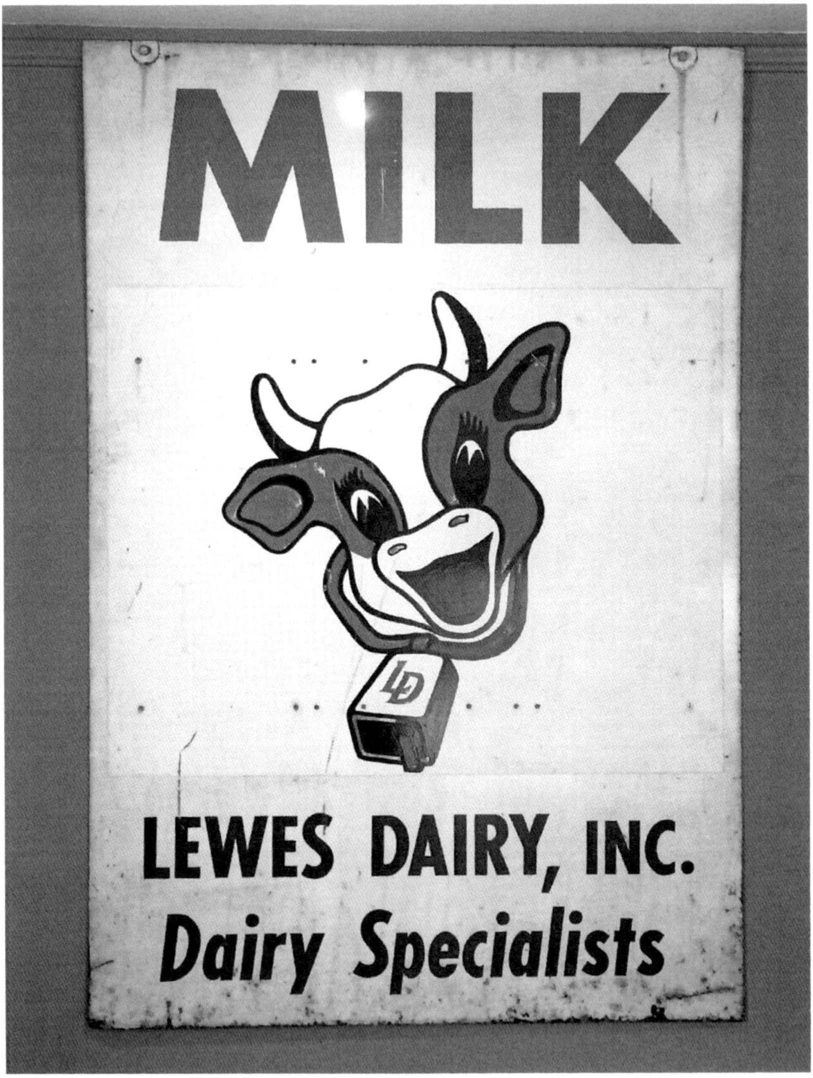

The Lewes Dairy logo, a belled and smiling cow. *Jack Clemons photo.*

in a bag tied to a stick and vigorously shaken until butter formed. What happens during the churning or shaking process is separation of the fat and liquid components in the cream. Fat globules become larger as they fuse together into bigger and bigger clumps, while the liquid and air are forced out, eventually producing a solid block of butter and the liquid byproduct known as "buttermilk." The butter is rinsed under cold water to remove any residual buttermilk, sprinkled lightly with salt and then formed into one-pound lumps to be stored in a wooden bucket or wrapped in waxed paper for sale.

Lewes Dairy, still in operation, was the first milk-bottling plant in the region to institute pasteurization, a sterilizing process designed to destroy any bacteria in the milk. They were also innovators in selling homogenized milk (where the fat is evenly dispersed throughout the liquid through a high-velocity stirring process). They pioneered steel bottle caps (ensuring quality and safety) and the gallon-sized milk container.

At the end of the day on the dairy farm, the cows were herded back from the meadow and returned to their stalls to be milked and fed once again before bedding down on a pile of straw. While some of the milking and processing operations have become mechanized, which significantly improved productivity, the number of dairies in the region has decreased over the past few decades. One positive result is that while the producers (both cows and farmers) have declined, more efficient practices have allowed the volume of dairy production to increase.

Some of the family names still associated with the dairy business in the region include Hopkins' Green Acres Farm in Lewes, Brittingham of Lewes Dairy, Vanderwende Farm Creamery in Greenwood and Warren's Rustic Acres Farm offering products under the Rehoboth Dairy label. From milk to ice cream, local cows still feed the residents of Southern Delaware.

Beer and Cider

Beer is proof God loves us and wants us to be happy.

—Benjamin Franklin

When European settlers arrived in the region, some of the most important skills they brought were cider and beer-making. Convinced that the water in rivers and streams was unsafe to drink, they immediately assembled the tools and ingredients to brew less dangerous beverages. Because this was before the time of quality-controlled municipal water supplies, they were quite right to use the brewing processes to purify the water that went into beer or to choose cider as an alternative to water.

The key ingredient in both beer and cider is some form of starch that will ultimately ferment. Apples were in ready supply for producing cider, while beer could be brewed from grains such as wheat, oats, corn and barley. Both cider and beer were produced in small quantities on most family farms. And it was once again the woman of the house who was responsible for making cider or beer, just as she was responsible for the laundry and milking chores.

During the colonial era in Southern Delaware, as well as across Europe, the term "cider" did not mean pressed apple juice but instead referred to what we today call "hard cider," an alcoholic drink of fermented apple pressings. Cider making required just three steps: grind or mill the apples into a pulp, press the pulp to extract the juice and store the juice for a period of time to allow fermentation to occur.

As settlements grew in size and numbers, a town tavern was constructed at a site near the center of commerce, typically a mill or water landing for boat traffic. Many tavern proprietors pressed and bottled cider for sale to their patrons, as well as operated a brewery or distillery to produce other beverages.

The most desirable grain for brewing beer was malted or germinated barley. Before sufficient supplies of barley were grown, brewers might turn to other grains, most often corn. The grains were cracked open and steeped in boiling water to extract the sugars, a process called mashing. This mixture, which developed the consistency of cooked oatmeal, was placed in a whiskey barrel that was set in a container to catch the strained liquid. The wooden staves of the barrel acted like a sieve, allowing the liquid to seep out and retaining the solids within to be used for animal feed. Alternatively, the mash and liquid were separated by pouring the mixture through a flannel bag.

Next, the collected liquid was transferred to a copper kettle and boiled for about two hours. Now slightly concentrated, this boiled mixture was mixed with hops, allowed to cool, combined with yeast and drained into wooden kegs to age for a few weeks before it was ready to drink. Not as high in alcohol as modern beer, this brew is closer to what we know as "near beer" and was often the beverage served at mealtimes to provide hydration and nourishment.

The steps involved in brewing beer haven't changed through the years, although large commercial breweries have mechanized many of the processes from mashing to bottling. In Southern Delaware, several local craft breweries

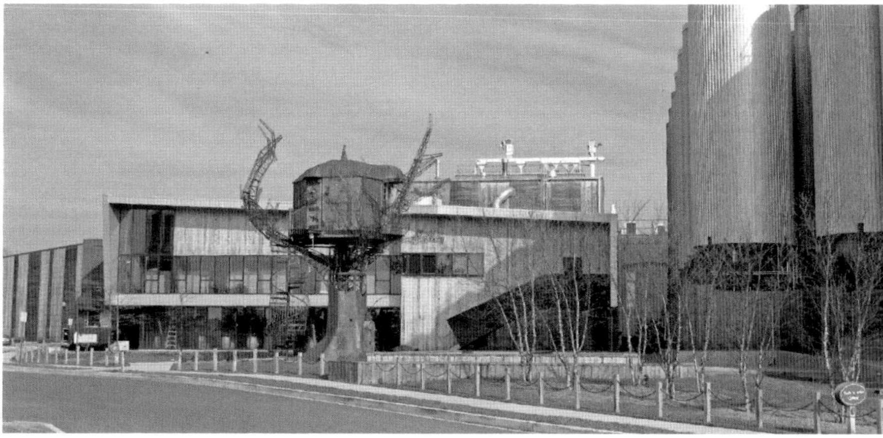

The somewhat off-centered Steampunk Treehouse outside the Dogfish Head Brewery in Milton, Delaware, today. *Jack Clemons photo.*

have recently emerged, emphasizing their focus on small, artisanal batches of beer, just like the farmers' wives produced in the eighteenth century.

One of the local breweries that has gained international fame is the curiously named Dogfish Head, so called after the town in Maine where founder Sam Calagione spent his childhood summers. When Dogfish Brewing & Eats opened in 1995, not only was it Delaware's first brewpub, but it was also the smallest commercial brewery in the country—so small, in fact, that its original batch of Shelter Pale Ale was brewed in twelve-gallon batches in tiny kegs equipped with propane burners.

As its reputation spread beyond Southern Delaware, orders started arriving from Pennsylvania; Washington, D.C.; and New Jersey. To commemorate the first six-pack sold out of the state of Delaware, Calagione imitated George Washington and rowed across the Delaware Bay to deliver his beer. Through a process of constant experimentation, Dogfish Head expanded its range of "off-centered beers" and relocated to Milton, Delaware, into a former cannery with enough space for all its product lines.

With names as unique as their products, the list of breweries in the region continues to grow. These are the breweries currently in operation in Southern Delaware, with a few more waiting in the wings to open their doors:

- 16 Mile Brewing, Georgetown
- 3rd Wave Brewing, Delmar
- Crooked Hammock Brewery, Lewes

- Dewey Beer Company, Dewey Beach
- Dogfish Head Craft Brewery, Milton
- Evolution Craft Brewing, Delmar
- Fordham Brewing, Dover
- Mispillion River Brewing, Milford
- Old Dominion Brewing, Dover

WINE

The first Europeans who came to North America were confident that this verdant region would be a perfect place to make wine. As they soon discovered, they were mistaken. Because of the significantly different environment, European grapevines brought by the settlers did not survive the native pests and diseases they encountered in the new country. Various experiments to establish vineyards in nearby Virginia and Pennsylvania failed completely. And despite his reputation as a wine connoisseur and amateur vintner, Thomas Jefferson also failed in his efforts to cultivate European grapes for winemaking.

For this reason, only imported wines from European countries such as France, Germany, Italy and Spain were found on the American table until the nineteenth century. One particular favorite during the early days of the colonies came from the Portuguese island of Madeira. Casks of Madeira wine not only survived the lengthy sea journeys to North America but also improved with age during the trip. In the mid-1700s, the practice of fortifying Madeira with brandy made it an even more popular choice.

Southern Delaware was not the site of a successful vineyard until the twentieth century, by which time publications about winemaking experiences in California's newly established vineyards and rigorous biological research into fungal diseases provided enterprising vintners with the tools to succeed.

Founded in 1987, Nassau Valley Vineyards in Lewes became the first commercial winery in the region. But before it could officially begin production and sales, the owners had to lobby the state legislature to repeal a law prohibiting farm-based vineyards. Since that time, Nassau has earned numerous awards for the many wines it blends from the Chardonnay, Cabernet and Merlot grapes it grows.

Pizzadili Winery in Felton, Delaware, planted its first grapevines in 1993 and has expanded to twelve different varieties. It produces a range of wines from a dry red table wine to a sweet white dessert wine it has named Delaware. Another recent addition to the winery inventory in Southern Delaware is Harvest Ridge, spanning the border between Delaware and Maryland in Marydel, Delaware. It opened to the public in 2013 and currently produces more than a dozen different wines, along with seasonal specialties such as Pumpkin Jack.

DISTILLERIES

The business of distilling alcoholic beverages began in Southern Delaware before the Revolutionary War and may have, in fact, helped the colonists build their courage to fight against the English king. Available raw materials for brandy included the many fruits growing wildly in the regions: grapes, plums, apples, blackberries, pears, cherries and peaches.

Another popular distilled drink was the morally ambiguous rum, the commerce behind which relied on the triangle trade route that included stops at slave-trading ports. The number of rum distilleries operating in the colonies during 1770 is estimated at more than 140, with production nearing 5 million gallons annually. Not every pint was consumed in the colonies, as many distilleries exported their rum across southern Europe, England and Ireland.

In *History of Delaware*, J. Thomas Scharf's detailed accounting of people and industry includes the names of various distilleries situated across the region. Some of these changed hands a few times but remained in operation from the seventeenth century through 1888. After the Civil War, distilleries continued to produce whiskey and brandy, the latter most notably from the abundant peach crops well into the last quarter of the nineteenth century.

Prohibition did not encourage distilleries to continue their operations, and at the same time, changes in the agricultural landscape offered more profitable enterprises for farmers and food processors. As a result, local distilleries began to disappear in the early twentieth century.

Recently, Southern Delaware has become home to a new breed of distillers. Beach Time Distilling in Lewes, Delaware Distilling Company and Dogfish Head Distillery in Rehoboth Beach and Painted Stave Distilling in Smyrna all produce hand-crafted spirits honoring the traditions of the trade and pushing the boundaries of flavor. Their skilled still-masters combine local ingredients to produce a unique collection of flavors, some available only in their tasting rooms. This is a list of their respective selections of small-batch spirits currently produced:

- Beach Time Distilling: Beach Fin Gin, Beach Fire Spiced Rum, Beach Gold Rum, Beach Ski Vodka, Beach Plum Rum and Beach Time Rum
- Delaware Distilling Company: Spiced Rum, Premium Gin and Premium Vodka
- Dogfish Head Distillery: Analog Vodka, Compelling Gin, Whole Leaf Gin, Brown Honey Rum and Peanut Butter Vodka
- Painted Stave Distilling: Diamond State Bourbon Whiskey, Diamond State Rye Whiskey, Candy Manor Gin, Silver Screen Vodka, Time Warp Espresso Vodka and Off the Hoof Scrapple Vodka

Recipes

Apple Cider

This recipe comes from Elizabeth Cleland's collection dating from 1755 and transcribed into modern English. It is a good illustration that immigrants from Scotland arrived in this country with knowledge of how to make apple cider using a mechanical press. Some helpful definitions: "hair bag" or "hair cloth" is another name for sackcloth or burlap; "isinglass" is made from a fish's air bladder and used as a clarifying agent; "bung" can refer to either the opening itself or the stopper to seal the opening in a cask.

To make Syder [sic]

When the Apples are ripe, pull them on a dry Day, and pound them in a Trough with wooden pounders, then put them in a Hair Bag, and press the Juice out of them; put it in a Brandy or white Wine Cask that is very sweet. Put in the Cask some slices of Apples and two Penny-worth of Isinglass; stop the Bung close, and bottle it in ten Months.

Rum-Glazed Chicken Wings

This is glazed with a spiced rum sauce, as seen in the color photo section.

12 pieces chicken wings
kosher salt
white pepper
2 tablespoons butter
2 chopped sage leaves
freshly ground nutmeg
⅓ cup chicken broth
½ cup spiced rum
salt and pepper, to taste

Dry chicken pieces and generously season with kosher salt and white pepper. Melt butter in a large skillet and add chicken pieces. Cook until well browned, turning a few times to keep from burning. Sprinkle with chopped sage and a few grates of fresh nutmeg from a microplane. Pour in chicken broth and rum, scraping up any browned bits. Reduce heat to very low and simmer until cooked through, about 15 minutes. Season to taste with salt and pepper.

Chapter 10

THE ROAD TO THE FUTURE

This culinary journey through Southern Delaware began with the region's early inhabitants, explorers and settlers. We spent some time in the colonial era visiting small family farms and watched how much changed economically with the growth of commercial agriculture in the eighteenth and nineteenth centuries. But we continued to eat the same foods we were growing for sale to outside markets, holding back enough to feed our families and still hunting a few rabbits and deer.

In the Victorian era, while the big-city elite made sure they had enough silverware for twelve-piece place settings, the less urban townspeople in Kent and Sussex Counties spent more time working than hosting fancy balls and entertainments. Some lovely examples of Victorian architecture still stand in towns like Lewes, Seaford, Millsboro and Bridgeville, but little of the trappings were seen in the menus of the day, with perhaps the notable exception of turtle or terrapin soup.

During the time of the Great Depression, this region was more protected from financial loss than the industrial centers in nearby cities like Wilmington and Baltimore. Most farmers did not need to stand in a bread line on a street corner to wait for a handout; they were able to grow enough for their families to eat and some to barter with neighbors for what else they might need. We kept eating chicken, baking bread and drinking milk.

Despite the condition of the economy, or perhaps because of it, changes erupted on the food front in the 1920s and 1930s. A variety of new convenience products and sweet treats appeared: Baby Ruth candy bars,

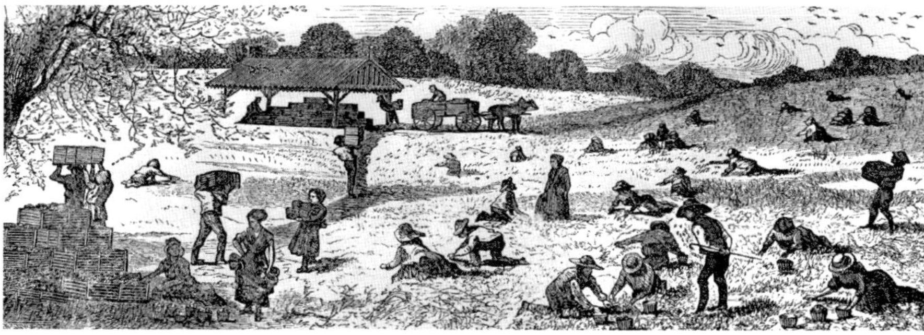

"Strawberry Picking Season," an illustration of the labor-intensive work involved in hand-picking Delaware strawberries. *Courtesy of the Delaware Public Archives.*

Yoo-Hoo chocolate drink, Reese's peanut butter cups, Pez candy, Hostess cakes, Kool-Aid drink mix, Peter Pan peanut butter, Spam potted meat and Velveeta. And as the woes of the Depression started to ease, many kitchens were modernized to include a welcome appliance: the refrigerator. Before long, frozen vegetables gained in popularity, some brands of which are still processed in nearby plants.

When World War II began, so did a proliferation of technological advances. While industries in Wilmington thrived with wartime demand for their products (gunpowder, cotton cloth, ships and steel), only a handful of Southern Delaware towns enjoyed additional prosperity because of the war: DuPont's plant in Seaford produced nylon for military parachutes, Dover's International Latex manufactured life boats and a branch of Triumph Explosives operated in Milford.

The Second World War caused a problem for farming families and commercial farms in Southern Delaware: a labor shortage. Across the region, draft-eligible men went into military service, and when demand for farm-related goods began to increase, especially for canned foods in the later years of the war, farm workers were in limited supply. One surprising solution came from the military base at Fort Miles (in what is now Cape Henlopen State Park outside of Lewes). From here, members of the German prisoner-of-war population were sent to work at nearby farms, helping with planting and harvest. According to several family histories, more than one foreign soldier stayed in the area or returned to Delaware after the war ended.

One effect of the war was inescapable, even for the highly productive local farmers: rationing. Introduced in 1940, the logic behind food rationing was to ensure that there was enough food to feed the men (and women) fighting for the country. First on the list were familiar staples such as bacon, butter and sugar, the last giving rise to the popularity of the artificial sweetener, saccharin, which local historian Hazel Brittingham lauded for giving her the ability to survive the war years without giving up her iced tea.

The next set of foods to be rationed were meat, fat, cheese and eggs, which encouraged the residents of small towns to alert their neighbors when any coveted supplies were delivered to the shops on Main Street. Hazel reported that when bacon showed up, everyone told everyone to hurry into town. Of course, this scarcity led to a number of creative approaches to "making do" with what was at hand. One national radio program, the *Kitchen Front*, asked listeners to contribute recipe ideas. Among the more unusual dishes shared were rosehip chutney, crow pie, sheep's head broth and squirrel tail soup. Sadly, they neglected to mention muskrat, so plentiful in nearby streams. At the same time, the government launched campaigns encouraging families to plant "Victory Gardens," hardly a new idea for the farm families of Southern Delaware.

After the end of the war, life returned to a new normal across the region. Some industries faded in the face of competition or consolidation, while

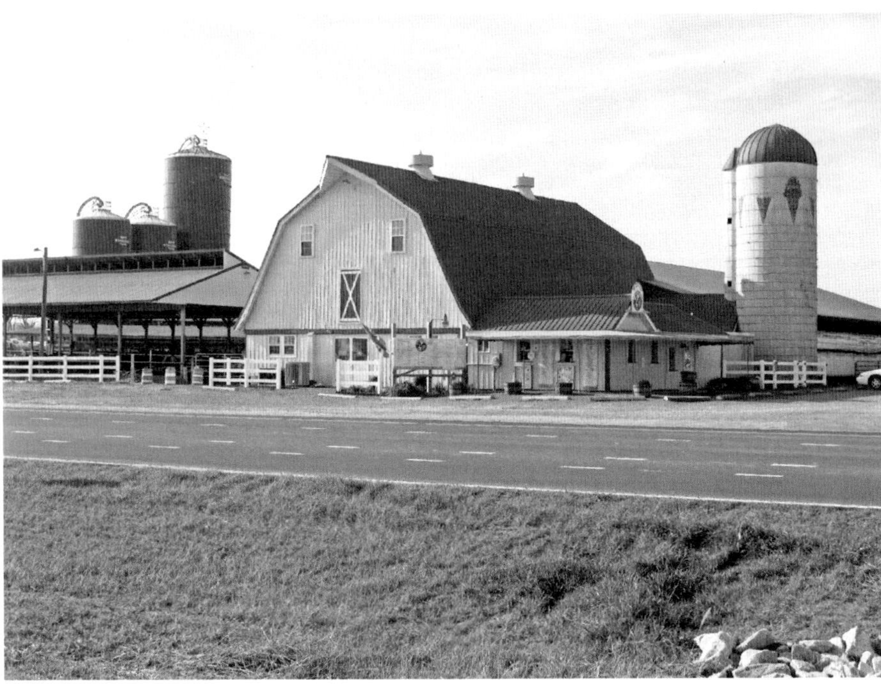

Hopkins Farm Creamery, where you can enjoy a scoop of homemade ice cream right from the cow to the cone, in Lewes, Delaware. *Jack Clemons photo.*

at the same time convenience-oriented manufactured food gained a firm foothold. The local groceries now stocked boxes of parboiled, fast-cooking Minute Rice and dozens of sugary breakfast cereals advertising television characters. We no longer baked bread but rather eagerly awaited the arrival of the Bond Bread delivery man with his enticing assortment of sliced breads and snacks. Through these changes, the Lewes Dairy continued morning doorstep deliveries of milk and cream, interrupted briefly when the owners were completing their military service.

And as if this level of convenience were not enough, enter the frozen TV dinner in its compartmentalized aluminum tray, perfectly sized to fit on a foldable metal stand placed in front of the television for comfortable viewing and dining. Copious amounts of salt, monosodium glutamate and sugar found their way into these prepared foods in order to make them palatable, although there was considerable debate about exactly what "meat" was in the "meatloaf" and "chopped sirloin steaks."

Oddly enough, along with an explosion of fast-food restaurant chains selling fried burgers and French fries came a new interest in low-calorie and low-fat foods. Soon, lower-fat and skim milk were bigger sellers than whole milk. Light or "lite" buttery spreads replaced butter on breakfast toast. Fat-free salad dressings and soups appeared, with formulations replacing fat with chemicals designed to introduce texture. Baked chips stacked in a cylindrical package replaced bags of fried potato chips, and an entire aisle was required to hold all the diet drinks stocked by most supermarkets.

Deep in the vast but quiet pockets of Southern Delaware, some families who lived in the region for generations might have added some of these conveniences to their diets, but the traditional favorites—steamed crabs, fried oysters, chicken and dumplings, stewed muskrat and more—never fell out of favor. Fresh tomatoes, corn, peaches and watermelon continued to appear on their tables in abundance every summer.

As this traditionally agricultural community continues to thrive, we are now watching a trend emerge in nearby urban areas and throughout the country. Foodies advise people to "eat local" and embrace the "slow food movement" that advocates maintaining culinary traditions and supporting small-scale farming. Isn't that the epitome of what has always been Southern Delaware's approach to food?

Who are the providers of "slow food" today? Travel to a farmers' market any day of the week across the region to meet them. Stop by Hopkins Creamery and visit the cows while you enjoy an ice cream cone. Buy a pint of the beloved Lewes Dairy Eggnog, which has gone on sale each holiday

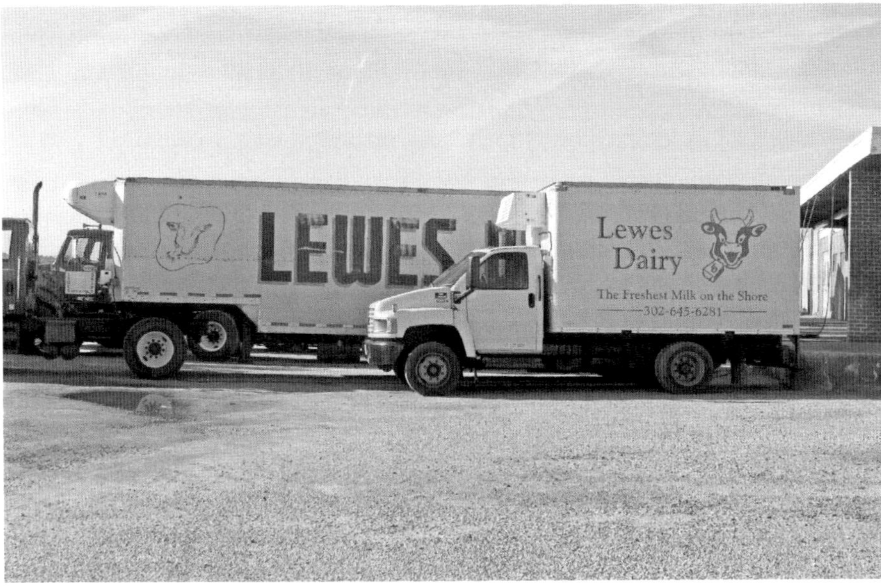

Despite being sold to Hy-Point Dairy in 2013, Lewes Dairy kept its familiar name and its signature eggnog recipe. *Jack Clemons photo.*

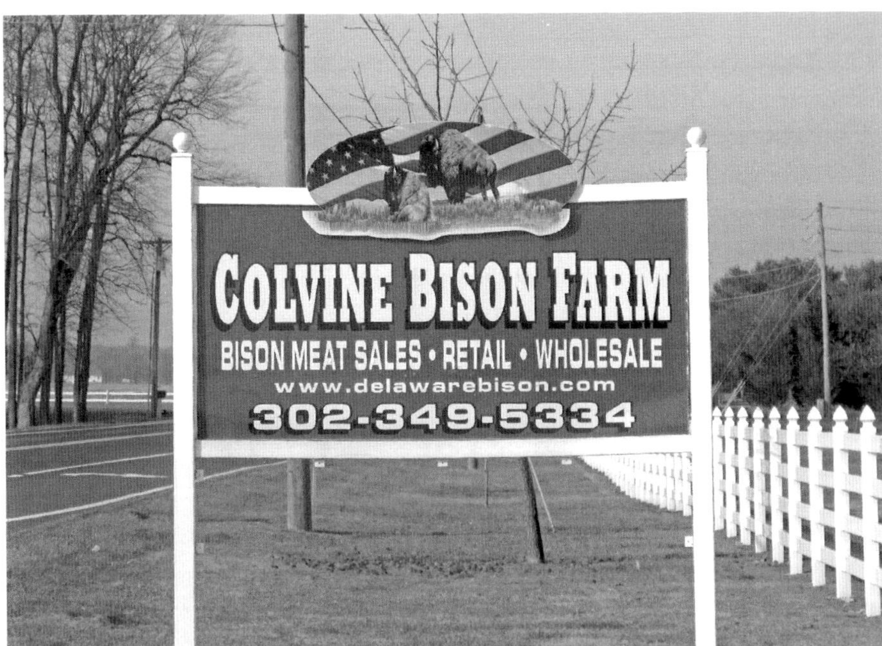

Bison still roam in Southern Delaware today, most notably at the Colvine Bison Farm in Greenwood. *Jack Clemons photo.*

season for almost seventy-five years. Attend a "farm to table" dinner hosted by one of our talented local chefs; the suppliers who made the meal possible might be seated next to you. Shop at one of the longstanding family-owned corner grocery stores that continue to sell local produce and milk. Dine at any of the regional restaurants that source their ingredients locally—from bison to chicken and fresh vegetables to artisanal bread and cheese.

As we began our story of the culinary history of Southern Delaware, full of the plenty of the land and sea, so, too, does the story end. Chickens are returning to a cage-free existence; cattle and bison once again graze local pastures; cows live contentedly in Cool Spring and Rehoboth Beach; peaches, apples, strawberries and blueberries are picked in nearby orchards; scrapple is made from a ninety-year-old recipe; oysters and crabs are returning to local waters in greater numbers; and colorful vegetables continue to thrive in the mild climate. From scrapple to beach plums, peaches to muskrat, the best from local farmers and fishermen has always been on the table in Southern Delaware.

RECIPES

Terrapin

This recipe comes from the Blue Hen's Chickens' Cook Book *of 1921 and resembles Fannie Farmer's earlier version. These instructions are far more concise than the two pages devoted to terrapin in Amelia Simmons's* 1796 American Cookery. *After the end of the Victorian era, turtle soup fell out of favor and is rarely seen on a menu today.*

Boil them until the shells come off easily and the nails pull out; remove the skin from the legs; cut into small pieces and carefully remove the sand bag and gall. To three good sized terrapins add six hard boiled eggs; mash the yolks into a powder and rub in one half pound of butter; when creamy and light add a heaping teaspoonful of flour; put into the chafing dish the meat and dressing; season with cayenne pepper and salt, and let them boil a minute or two. Just before serving add wine to taste, and if desired a very little mace.

Bison Rib-Eye

These elegant steaks, seen in the color section, deliver a clean, meaty flavor from pasture-raised bison.

olive oil
2 bison rib-eye steaks
garlic or onion powder
black pepper

Rub olive oil across both sides of the steak and sprinkle with seasonings. Brush the grate with vegetable oil or nonstick cooking spray. Preheat the grill on high for at least 10 minutes before cooking. Place the steaks over the direct flame and cook for 1 minute on each side. Reduce the temperature to medium and move the steaks away from the direct heat. Cook another four minutes on each side. Place the steaks on a platter, loosely covered with foil and allow to rest for about 10 minutes before serving. Yield: 2 servings.

Appendix I
HOW COOKBOOKS TELL OUR STORIES

The contents, omissions and styles of instruction found in a cookbook can yield valuable insights into the lives of the people who wrote it and the audience for whom it was written. The emergence of an American cookbook tradition has its roots in the cultural evolution of the new country but can trace its beginnings as far back as the hieroglyphics found in Egyptian tombs. A cookbook, defined as a collection of instructions for cooking food, is often sorted into types of menu items, such as appetizers or desserts. Alternatively, a cookbook may be organized by specific ingredients, such as fish, meats and vegetables. The explicit directions for an individual dish is known as a recipe, archaically seen written as "receipt."

As you may imagine, recipes have existed in the oral tradition for as long as humans have been eating. Recipes were found in a number of ancient sites and documents, from the ruins of Pompeii to the early Greek writings of Athenaeus, whose second-century treatise is in the form of a dialogue between epicures attending a banquet. A master chef who served the thirteenth-century court of Kublai Kahn documented hints and tips about eating and drinking for his contemporaries.

Within a hundred years, manuscripts on vellum scrolls captured the recipes of the master cooks of Richard II. The complete text of this fascinating tome, *The Forme of Cury*, is available for reference online through the efforts of Project Gutenburg. One section details a feast hosted by the king and the Duke of Lancaster in 1387; their menu called for the following list of supplies: "14 oxen lying insalt, 120 carcas of shepe fresh, 140 pigges, 210 gees, 400 rabbits, 11 thousand eggs." By the time the printing press came into use in the late fifteenth century, cookbooks had begun to appear in almost every country.

Many of these early books were written by chefs responsible for preparing meals for royalty or members of the privileged class of people they served. Because of the strict enforcement of class structure, these also included instructions on how to properly run the kitchen, with guidelines on specific job responsibilities, detailing the behavior required of servants and household staff. One of the most well-known collections of haute cuisine dishes was written by a man considered to be the first celebrity chef, Frenchman Antonin Carême, who published the lavishly illustrated *L'art de la Cuisine* in the early 1800s.

If newly arrived European colonists to North America carried a cookbook among their belongings, it most likely was *The Compleat Housewife* by Eliza Smith, published in London in 1727 and reprinted eighteen times in London during the following fifty years. The cover text describes the vast scope of this book:

> *Being a collection of several hundred approved receipts, in cookery, pastry, confectionery, preserving, pickles, cakes, creams, jellies, made wines, cordials. And also bills of fare for every month of the year. To which is added, a collection of nearly two hundred family receipts of medicines; viz. drinks, syrups, salves, ointments, and many other things of sovereign and approved efficacy in most distempers, pains, aches, wounds, sores, etc. never before made publick in these parts; fit either for private families, or such public-spirited gentlewomen as would be beneficent to their poor neighbours.*

This volume was reprinted in Williamsburg in 1742, designed for women looking to keep up with London's culinary trends. The publisher's only attempt to Americanize it was to delete certain recipes, "the ingredients or material for which are not to be had in this country," but for the most part, the book was not adjusted to American kitchens or available foods found only in North America at the time. Another English cookbook, Hannah Glasse's *The Art of Cookery*, was first issued in 1747 in London and subsequently reprinted in Alexandria, Virginia, in 1805. This was touted as the most popular cookbook in 1776, and copies appeared in the libraries of both Benjamin Franklin and George Washington.

Although Susannah Carter's *The Frugal Housewife or Complete Woman Cook* appeared in London later than Glasse's book, hers was one of the first to appear in the new colonies. In 1772, a Boston reprint included two plates drawn by Paul Revere as the frontispiece, and an 1803 New York reprint included more than a dozen new recipes featuring American-based dishes and ingredients, such as Indian pudding and cornmeal mush.

Each of these books contained many of the same recipes, written in exactly the same way and organized in the same fashion. The first truly American cookbook did not appear until 1796, when *American Cookery* by Amelia Simmons was published in Hartford, Connecticut. If imitation is the sincerest form of flattery, Simmons was certainly admired, as numerous reprints of her collection appeared over the next fifty years, some without her name cited as the author.

Although Simmons was unabashed about borrowing recipes previously printed by other writers, she was the first American woman to write a cookbook and the earliest source of uniquely American dishes. Among the innovations she featured were puddings of crookneck or winter squash, how to prepare Jerusalem artichokes, turkey served with cranberry sauce, soft gingerbread cakes and the suggestion to use corncobs for smoking bacon. Almost every Thanksgiving Day menu today includes an Amelia Simmons invention: the combination of cream, eggs, spices and stewed pumpkin, served originally as a pudding and eventually baked into pie.

A few years later in this country, Simmons was followed by Mary Randolph's *The Virginia Housewife or, Methodical Cook*, issued in 1824 and reprinted in 1860. Her approach to managing a household, as well as the inclusion of dishes inspired by plantation living, made her work popular enough to support the publication of nineteen different editions prior to the start of the Civil War. Randolph's book might not have been as useful for the residents of Southern Delaware, as many of her guidelines were based on the slaveholding practices of Virginia, a practice already abolished here.

Early in the Victorian era, another American woman, Sarah Joseph Hale, published an important cookbook, originally titled *The Good Housekeeper, or, the Way to Live Well, and to Be Well While We Live*. As the editor of two popular lifestyle magazines—*Ladies Magazine* (1827–36) and *Godey's Lady's Book* (1837–77)—Hale was already a well-known and influential arbiter of taste for women in the newly established United States. Her preface to the second edition of her book on American cookery clearly outlines her philosophy: "Bear in mind that in preparing food, three things are to be united, the promotion of health, the study of economy, and the gratification of taste." Although every homemaker already knew how to bake bread, this is the earliest appearance of a recipe for baking a yeast-raised wheat-flour loaf of bread.

The Civil War inspired Maria Moss to publish *A Poetical Cookbook* in 1864, the proceeds of which were advertised to subsidize the medical costs for Union soldiers. This charity-based cookbook trend has persisted through today, with religious congregations, civic organizations, schools, libraries and community associations publishing collections to raise money for various causes and construction projects.

A major shift in cookbooks arrived at the end of the nineteenth century, when Fanny Merritt Farmer published the *Boston Cooking-School Cook Book* in 1896. Instead of recipes written in the form of a paragraph, often without specifying precise amounts of each ingredient, guidance on cooking times or temperatures, Farmer's book was the origin of a scientific approach to cooking. She designed a format, still in use today, listing the required quantities of each ingredient, followed by sequential instructions for each step in the preparation.

One reversal of this focus on scientific form and specificity is seen in *The Blue Hen's Chickens' Cook Book* published in Milford, Delaware, in 1921. Resembling the earlier format found in Simmons's book, these were written in paragraphs, combining instructions and vague guidelines as to ingredients—for example, several advise to "chop the clams" without indicating how many or how small. The introduction boasted that the region "has for two hundred years been famous the world over for the lusciousness of its viands and the excellence of its cooking." And the recipes collected came from "only those well-known for their cooking." Each of the sections appears after a lighthearted epigraph, and the opening pages feature instructions on "To Cook a Husband."

In addition to the ongoing publication of many charity-based cookbooks, others reflected the trends in available resources. One familiar example is the variety of "ration book" cookbooks and pamphlets published during the 1940s. These included patriotically named foods like "liberty loaf," which combined cooked oatmeal, cornmeal and potatoes to supplement flour, which was in scarce supply. Cookbooks of this era always had a section of "low point" recipes, which could be made with ingredients available for the lowest quantity of ration-book points.

After the war, an explosion in generally available ingredients and new food products began to spawn cookbooks published by kitchen tool manufacturers and food processors with the purpose of teaching people how to use their products. From rennet to tapioca, Campbell's soups to Rumford's baking powder, everything new on the grocery shelf needed a guidebook. From waffle irons to toasters, mixers and blenders, every new or improved kitchen appliance required its own cookbook.

As people became more health conscious, cookbooks began to include calorie counts and nutritional content for ingredients in the prepared dishes. Traditional recipes appeared next to "lighter" versions of the same dish, substituting lower-calorie ingredients (e.g., low-fat milk instead of whole milk) or changing the cooking process to baking or oven-frying instead of frying in an oil-filled skillet.

One of the most cherished cookbook traditions in Southern Delaware came from Elaine Mitchell. She began as a social-scene reporter in the 1970s with her newspaper column "Looking at Lewes." Each week, she described a social gathering, with a focus on the food served at the event. As she became more popular, the newspaper added another column by her, "What's Cooking," which featured not only recipes but also the names of the home cooks or local chefs who created them.

Later in the decade, she began working with artist Carole Smith, who illustrated cookbooks, notecards and engagement calendars with pen-and-ink sketches of local sights to accompany Elaine's recipes. She published several cookbooks, most notably *What's Cooking in Lewes*, which was reprinted five times, selling almost nine thousand copies. Her untimely death in 1982 left her followers grateful to have her books in their collections. Elaine's voice can be heard in her obvious appreciation for the local bounty and her celebration of local cooks in the lighthearted summaries at the end of each recipe, as in her remark about Bar-B-Que Hamburger: "So easy to do you could let your kids take over the kitchen to fix this simple recipe."

Through the years, cookbooks have become valuable references, not only as a way to understand what ingredients were available and how specific dishes were prepared but also as a way to provide insight into the cultural milieu at the time of their publication.

Appendix II
FARMS AND MARKETS IN SOUTHERN DELAWARE

During the growing season, towns across the region hold weekly farmers' markets. Some assemble at the town park, while others set up in a parking lot. No matter the location, these sites are where farmers showcase their freshest products. Depending on the market, you will find everything from fruits and vegetables to meat and seafood. A few of the markets include vendors who sell prepared foods, including baked goods, dried pastas, salads and sandwiches.

- Bethany Beach: Sundays 8:00 a.m. to noon, Garfield Parkway and Pennsylvania Avenue, June–August
- Dover: Wednesdays 11:00 a.m. to 3:00 p.m., 27 Lookerman Way, June–September
- Fenwick Island: Mondays and Fridays 8:00 a.m. to noon, East Essex Street and Coastal Highway, June–September
- Georgetown: Wednesdays 3:00 p.m. to 6:00 p.m., 16 Mile Brewery, 413 South Bedford Street, May–September
- Lewes: Saturdays 8:00 a.m. to noon, George H.P. Smith Park by Blockhouse Pond, May–November
- Milton: Fridays 3:00 p.m. to 6:00 p.m., Union and Magnolia Streets or Dogfish Head Brewery, April–October
- Rehoboth Beach: Tuesdays noon to 4:00 p.m., Grove Park on Rehoboth Avenue, May–October

- Milford: Saturdays 9:00 a.m. to 1:00 p.m., Riverwalk Park at South Walnut Street, May–October
- Sea Colony: Wednesdays 8:00 a.m. to noon, Marketplace at Sea Colony Shopping Center on Route 1, June–August

The Delaware Department of Agriculture maintains an extensive database of producers who invite the public to visit, whether for tours, tastings or a chance to pick your own fruit. For additional details, its website is de.gov/buylocal.

BIBLIOGRAPHY

Allmond, Frances. *The First State: First Lady's Recipe Book*. Wilmington, DE: Charles Printing Company, 1975.

Better Homes and Gardens Heritage Cookbook. Des Moines, IA: Meredith Corporation, 1975.

Boyd, William H. *The Delaware State Directory and Gazetteer for 1874–75*. Wilmington, DE: Commercial Printing Company, 1874.

Brown, Fiona Young. *A Culinary History of Kentucky*. Charleston, SC: Arcadia Publishing, 2014.

Carlisle, Nancy, and Melinda Talbot Nasardinov. *America's Kitchens*. Boston: Historic New England, 2008.

Carter, Richard B. *Clearing New Ground: The Life of John G. Townsend, Jr.* Wilmington: Delaware Heritage Press, 2001.

Carter, Susannah. *The Frugal Housewife Or, Complete Woman Cook*. Boston: Edes and Gill, 1772. Facsimile reprint by the American Antiquarian Society, Kansas City, MO: Andrews McMeel Publishing, 2013.

Caulk, Pat, and Grace Caulk. *Cows, Crops and Causes: Delaware Farmlife in the 1900s.* Mansfield, OH: Book Masters, 2000.

Cleland, Elizabeth. *A New and Easy Method of Cooking.* Edinburgh, Scotland: Gordon, Wright, Willison and Bruce, 1755.

Dozier, Herbert L. *Recipes for Cooking Muskrat Meat: Wildlife Leaflet 229.* Chicago, IL: United States Department of the Interior Fish and Wildlife Service, 1943.

Farmer, Fannie Merritt. *The Boston Cooking-School Cook Book.* Boston: Little, Brown and Company, 1896.

Federal Writers' Project of the Works Progress Administration for the State of Delaware. *Delaware: A Guide to the First State.* New York: Viking Press, 1938.

Fredericks, Anthony D. *The Secret Life of Clams: The Mysteries and Magic of Our Favorite Shellfish.* New York: Skyhorse Publishing, 2014.

Glasse, Hannah. *The Art of Cookery.* Alexandria, VA: Cottom & Stewart, 1805. Facsimile reprint, Bedford, MA: Applewood Books, 1997.

Hale, Sarah Joseph. *The Good Housekeeper.* Boston: Otis, Broaders, 1841. Facsimile reprint, Mineola, NY: Dover Publications, 1996.

Hancock, Harold Bell. *Delaware During the Civil War.* Wilmington: Historical Society of Delaware, 1961.

Hanna, James Milton. *More Tales from Delaware Bay.* Little Creek, DE: Cherokee Books, 2002.

Harris, Joy Sheffield. *A Culinary History of Florida.* Charleston, SC: Arcadia Publishing, 2014.

Inglenook Magazine. The Inglenook Cook Book. Elgin, IL: Brethren Publishing House, 1919.

Kee, Ed. *Delaware Farming.* Charleston, SC: Arcadia Publishing, 2007.

———. *Saving Our Harvest: The Story of the Mid-Atlantic Region's Canning and Freezing Industry.* Baltimore, MD: CTI Publications, 2006.

Kelly, Ian. *Cooking for Kings: The Life of Antonin Carême.* New York: Walker & Company, 2003.

Metropolitan Life Insurance Company. *The Metropolitan Life Cook Book.* New York: self-published, 1924.

Milford New Century Club. *The Blue Hen's Chickens' Cook Book.* Milford, DE: Milford Chronicle Publishing Company, 1921.

Moss, Maria. *A Poetical Cookbook.* Philadelphia, PA: Caxton Press, 1864.

Munroe, John A. *Colonial Delaware.* Millwood, NY: KTO Press, 1978.

1919 Directory of Canners in the United States. Washington, D.C.: National Canners Association, 1919.

Norwood, John R. *We Are Still Here!* Moorestown: Native New Jersey Publications, 2007.

Pierce, Charles, ed. *The Colonial Williamsburg Tavern Cookbook.* New York: Clarkson Potter/Publishers, 2001.

Porter, Frank. *The Nanticoke.* New York: Chelsea House Publishers, 1987.

Randolph, Mary. *The Virginia Housewife: Or Methodical Cook.* Philadelphia, PA: E.H. Butler & Company, 1860. Facsimile reprint, New York: Dover Publications, 1993.

Rendle, Ellen, and Constance J. Cooper. *Delaware in Vintage Postcards.* Charleston, SC: Arcadia Publishing, 2001.

Roundtree, Helen C., Wayne E. Clark and Kent Mountfort. *John Smith's Chesapeake Voyages, 1607–1609.* Charlottesville: University of Virginia Press, 2007.

Scharf, J. Thomas. *History of Delaware, 1609–1888.* Philadelphia, PA: Historical Society of Delaware, 1888.

Shields, John. *The Chesapeake Bay Cookbook.* N.p.: Addison-Wesley Publishing Company, 1990.

Simmons, Amelia. *American Cookery.* Hartford, CT: Hudson & Goodwin, 1796. Facsimile reprint, New York: Oxford University Press, 1958.

Speck, Frank G. *The Nanticoke Community of Delaware.* New York: AMS Press, 1915.

Stead, Jennifer. *Food & Cooking in 18th Century Britain.* N.p.: English Heritage, 1985.

Weaver, William Woys. *Country Scrapple.* Mechanicsburg, PA: Stackpole Books, 2003.

Williams, William H. *Delmarva's Chicken Industry: 75 Years of Progress.* Georgetown, DE: Delmarva Poultry Industry, 1998.

———. *Slavery and Freedom in Delaware, 1639–1865.* Wilmington, DE: Scholarly Resources, 1996.

INDEX

ABOUT THE AUTHOR

Denise Clemons has been cooking since she was old enough to hold a whisk, evolving from mother's helper to family chef to passionate food writer and instructor. She began her career in the technology industry after graduating from Vassar College with a BA in biopsychology. She spent twenty years in executive leadership before leaving the corporate world to pursue her interests in the nonprofit arena. She earned an MA in writing from Johns Hopkins University, majoring in poetry.

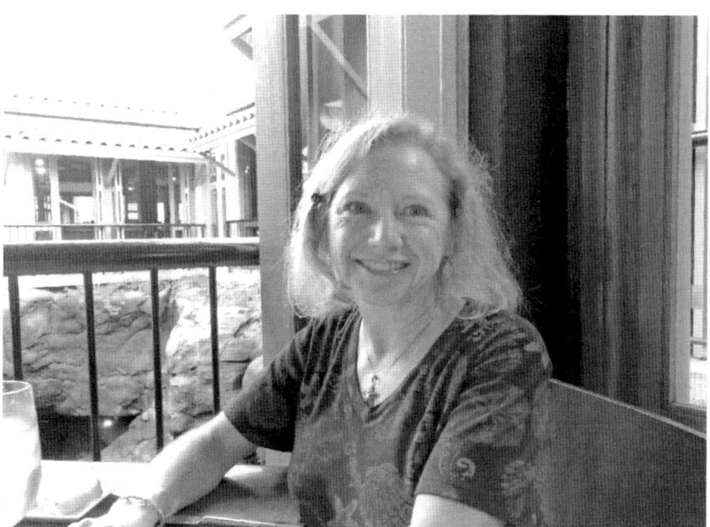

Denise and her husband, Jack, retired to Lewes, Delaware, where they live with their two cats, Virgil and Allie. For the past ten years, Denise has written "Cape Flavors," a weekly food column for the home cook. In addition to her interest in food, she also serves on the boards of a number of nonprofit organizations, including the Daughters of the American Revolution and the Eastern Shore Writers Association. In addition to food writing, her nonfiction, fiction and poetry have been published in journals, chapbooks and anthologies.

Denise regularly offers nutrition workshops, cooking demonstrations and presentations on topics related to food and history to audiences throughout the mid-Atlantic region.

Visit us at
www.historypress.net

This title is also available as an e-book